THE «COMEDIA LACRIMOSA»

and

SPANISH ROMANTIC DRAMA

(1773-1865)

JOAN LYNNE PATAKY KOSOVE

THE «COMEDIA LACRIMOSA»
and
SPANISH ROMANTIC DRAMA

(1773-1865)

TAMESIS BOOKS LIMITED
LONDON

Colección Támesis
SERIE A - MONOGRAFIAS LXVII

Depósito legal: M. 12127.—1978
Printed in Spain by SELECCIONES GRÁFICAS (EDICIONES)
Paseo de la Dirección, 52 - Madrid-29

for

TAMESIS BOOKS LIMITED
LONDON

To my husband Tony and children Andrew and Alexis.

CONTENTS

PREFACE

> Nevertheless, according to the few lights that remain to us, we may say that the Eighteenth Century, notwithstanding all its Error and Vices has been, of all that are past, the most honorable to human Nature.
>
> John Adams to Thomas Jefferson, from Quincy, November 13, 1815.

This book is the first critical and scholar'y examination of the philosophical bases and dramatic techniques of the sentimental comedy in Spain.[1] A few studies exist that treat Jovellanos' *El delincuente honrado,* concentrating on its relationship to Diderot's theories of «le genre sérieux.»[2]

On the other hand, extensive studies have been done on the English sentimental comedy: Ernest Bernbaum, *The Drama of Sensibility: A Sketch of the History of English Sentimental Comedy and Domestic Tragedy 1696-1780* (Cambridge, Mass.: Harvard University Press, 1925); on the French *comédie larmoyante*: Ferdinand Brunetière, «L'Evolution du drame bourgeois,» in his *Les époques du théâtre français 1636-1850* (Paris: Librairie Hachette, n.d.); Gustave Lanson, *Nivelle de la Chaussée et la comédie larmoyante,* 2nd ed. (1903; rpt. Geneva: Slatkine Reprints, 1970); C. Lenient, *La comédie en France au XVIIIᵉ siècle,* 2 vols. (Paris: Librairie Hachette, 1888); and on the German *bürgerliche Trauerspiel*: Arthur Eloesser, *Das burgerliche Drama: Seine Geschichte im 18. und 19. Jahrhundert,* 2nd ed. (1898; rpt. Geneva: Slatkine Reprints, 1970).

Unlike the studies cited above, the focus of which is either primarily historic or comparative, this work makes a detailed analysis of individual plays

---

[1] I. L. McClelland's book *Spanish Drama of Pathos 1750-1808* (Toronto: University of Toronto Press, 1970, vol. II), studies the evolution of Low Tragedy in Spain in the eighteenth century, but her approach is historic rather than philosophic. The *comedias lacrimosas* that are mentioned are studied for the most part, not for the philosophic, thematic and technical innovations they bring to drama, but rather as imitations or translations of foreign plays.

[2] See, for example, José M. Caso González, «*El delincuente honrado,* drama sentimental» in his *La poética de Jovellanos* (Madrid: Prensa Española, 1972), pp. 193-234, John H. R. Polt, «Jovellanos' *El delincuente honrado,*» *Rom. Rev.,* L (1959), 170-190, and Jean Sarrailh, «Á Propos du *Delincuente honrado* de Jovellanos» in *Mélanges d'Études Portugaises offerts à M. Georges Le Gentil* (Lisbon: Instituto para a Alta Cultura, 1949), pp. 337-351.

and isolates both the purposes and methods of the authors. These purposes and methods are related to the general philosophic character of the eighteenth century and to specific elements such as the growth of sentimentality in European thought and narrative literature. The *comedia lacrimosa* was a transitional form in an epoch of transition. It was the vehicle by which the way was prepared for the Romantic school in the Spanish theater, making the middle-class, which had previously been presented only in «laughing» comedy, the center of concern in serious drama. Thus my final chapter will examine the thematic, philosophic and technical elements of the *comedia lacrimosa* that anticipated Spanish Romantic drama. This study differs from any that have preceeded it both in its orientation, which is philosophic, and its method, which builds its conclusions upon detailed plot analyses of the individual plays that make up the genre being studied.

Since the majority of these *comedias lacrimosas* exist today only in highly inaccessible antique broadside editions and because there is so little published about them, I have felt it necessary to include some account of the plot content of the plays treated in this study. In some instances I have included actual summaries in order that the reader might see the types of situations the dramatists utilized to present the bourgeois, didactic and lachrymose material that is the main object of my interest in Chapters IV through IX. The aspects of these sentimental comedies that foreshadow Romantic drama will be studied in the final chapter.

Although I have of course quoted from specific editions of these *comedias lloronas,* it is often difficult to say what editions they are since most of them contain no reference to the publisher, or the place or date of publication. The reader will find information about the various known editions in my Bibliography. Throughout this book, I have faithfully reproduced both the spelling and the punctuation of passages quoted from the late eighteenth century and early nineteenth century broadsides and other play texts.

«Millstones»
Wyncote, Pennsylvania

JOAN L. PATAKY KOSOVE.

ACKNOWLEDGEMENTS

A very special obligation is due Dr. Russell P. Sebold of the University of Pennsylvania, a distinguished critic of eighteenth century Spanish literature. Professor Sebold suggested to me the need for a detailed work examining the contributions of the *comedia lacrimosa* to Spanish Romantic drama. I am greatly indebted to him for the very valuable and gracious assistance he gave me in the writing of this book.

I should like to thank my devoted professor and friend, Dr. Augusta Espantoso-Foley, for her most careful reading of the manuscript and her excellent recommendations. I am also in Professor Gonzalo Sobejano's debt for his helpful suggestions.

I wish to acknowledge the assistance of Dr. William McKnight of the University of North Carolina faculty and Mr. L. C. Scarborough and his staff in the Photographic Service at the same institution in obtaining Xerox copies of the the editions of many *comedias lacrimosas* found in the library of their institution.

This study has been supported in part by a grant from the Romance Language Publication Fund of the University of Pennsylvania.

Chapter I

SENTIMENTALISM IN EUROPEAN THOUGHT

AND NARRATIVE LITERATURE

The final decades of the seventeenth century and the first few of the eighteenth marked the beginning of a period in Western thought that has, perhaps, just run its course. The «uncertainty, or indeterminacy principle» in science, borne of Heisenberg's attempt to observe electron movements, opened the door to a profound questioning of empiricism and science which has reached its peak in the second half of the twentieth century. The *id*, discovered by Freud, and subsequently made the hero in its epic struggle with the *ego* seems to have failed modernity, which, free to feel and express everything, laments the lack of meaning as we turn to a new therapy of existential analysis. The scarcity of resources that support life systems and the failure of multi-national monetary and trade systems now call into question the belief in continual progress and man's claim to material ease.

But the later part of the seventeenth century and the eighteenth were ages full of optimism about the nature of man and the powers of science and its methodology. The philosophic, scientific and artistic thrust of that age either laid the groundwork for or reacted to the transfer of power from the aristocracy to the middle-class and all that was authoritarian or *a priori* came under scrutiny. That transfer led to a reversal of scientific, philosophic, religious, political and economic beliefs. Man was set free to feel and to express.[1]

In science the move was from deduction to inductive reasoning and empirical experimentation, which demanded the use of the senses and the observation of nature. In philosophy the emphasis again was on sensation as the conduit to knowledge, with a concomitant increase in the importance of individual experience.

---

[1] The move from scolasticism to empiricism, the move from deductive to inductive reasoning, the fascination of man with himself and his surroundings all play a part in what I call in the text «setting man free.» The beginning of these moves in modern European history is to be found in the fourteenth rather than the eighteenth century. But while the ideas and impulses stirred in the early European Renaissance, it was in the eighteenth century that these ideas would be widely circulated and utilized in the transference of power to the middle-class.

15

But the «human understanding,» of which John Locke wrote in 1690, would do more than explain how man came to know; it would reinforce a method of dealing with nature that would allow man to harmonize, if not exploit it, and derive from science material wealth that would promise an ease and happiness of which the common man had not yet dared to dream. Further, man's observation of nature would stir feelings and deep emotions heretofore in disfavor but now proudly claimed as his right, which in turn prepared the way for a humanitarian, fraternal, and sympathetic age.

Economics kept consistent pace with all these changes, as the fetters of a mercantile system that strangled real wealth with a belief in gold as wealth (since authority was confused with truth) gave way to a belief in *laissez-faire* economics and free trade, which blessed the natural competitive and acquisitive spirit of man.

In all of this vast panorama of ideas and expression, I view art as reactive. This is not to assign the literature of the age to a subordinate role, because without modes to suggest the implications and application of ideas in the affairs of men all philosophy and science would be stillborn. Bacon, Newton and Locke command the attention of students because their ideas and methodologies both raised and attempted to answer important questions. But most important, they command mankind's attention because they told us to open our eyes, engage our senses, to initiate our quest for truth, not from authority, but from ourselves, and these commands were embraced because they coincided with the aspirations of humanity with which literature is deeply concerned. From all this intellectual turbulence the modern age was born.

When I speak of the birth of the modern age in the Western world, I mean the period when the power to effect great events moved into the hands of the middle-class, when the means to effect material change became largely scientific, and when the stabilization of society began to require a broad consensus. The *comedia lacrimosa,* in its concern for the middle-class and their conventions, reflects the major currents of thought in the eighteenth century. It exemplifies the change of literary tastes and moral tendencies that are part of the general changes of thought and perception in the Age of Enlightenment.

As the middle-class emerged into its position of pre-eminence and became the class from which consensus had to be sought, it became for writers both a center of interest and a target for manipulation. Writers reached for a means suasion and began to use emotion to confirm beliefs. We call this device sentimentalism.

Sentimentalism appeared in literature in the very beginning of the eighteenth century and brought with it an impulse toward social reform. Literature became more ethical. Its aim was moral; it became didactic and dogmatic. The sentimental drama, essay, poetry and novel reflected the morals and customs of the times. The authors were writing for a public intensely interested in political, economic and social matters. The new forms of literature were addressed to a middle-class public. The bourgeoisie became the center of concern. These genres not only presented an exaltation of middle-class life but an attack on social prejudices and injustices. Their aim was to correct vice by means of sentiment and, as a result, there is a predominance of feeling, pity and emotion in these works.

The first genre which reflected this new wave of sentimentalism, and the genre with which I will be primarily concerned in this work, was drama. Just as the intellectual leadership of the eighteenth century belonged to England, so too did the literary and artistic supremacy. «La civilisation du XVIII° et du XIX° siècle sera essentiellement un phénomène anglais.»[2] Colley Cibber's *Love's Last Shift* (1696) marked the beginning of sentimental comedy.

Shortly thereafter, sentimentalism became prominent in other genres. It appeared in the sentimental essays of Addison and Steele. The aim of *The Tatler* (1709-1711) and *The Spectator* (1711-12; 1714) was moral. The purpose of *The Tatler* was to recommend truth, honor and virtue. As in sentimental comedy social justices are reproved by appealing to the tender heart of virtue. «To be apt to shed tears,» said Steele, «is a sign of great as well as little spirit» (*Tatler*, No. 68).[3] «That calm and elegant satisfaction which the vulgar call melancholy, is the true and proper delight of men of knowledge and virtue» (*Tatler*, No. 89, II, 278).

Addison and Steele wrote about theater. Steele criticized the satiric aspects of comedy. He said plays were needed «whence it is impossible to return without strong impressions of honor and humanity» (*Tatler*, Introduction, I, xxii). Rousseau attacked comedy on similar grounds forty years later in his *Lettre à d'Alembert sur les spectacles*.

Steele spoke of the theater's effect on the manners of the age: «...the theatre has much the same effect on the manners of the age, as the bank on the credit of the nation» (*Tatler*, No. 12, I, 111); and of the moral influence of theater: «It is not the business of a good play to make every man a hero; but it certainly gives him a livelier sense of virtue and merit than he had when he entered the theatre» (*Tatler*, No. 99, II, 334). *The Spectator* also expressed the belief that the theater could reform customs and contribute to the progress of the morality of the masses: «Were our *English* Stage but half so virtuous as that of the *Greeks* or *Romans*, we should quickly see the Influence of it in the Behavior of all the Politer Part of Mankind... Were our plays subject to proper Inspections and Limitations, we might not only pass away several of our vacant Hours in the highest Entertainment; but should always rise from them wiser and better than we sat down to them» (Addison in *The Spectator*, No. 446).[4]

These moral essays advanced other theories in harmony with sentimental comedy. Not only did they exalt didacticism, morality, feeling and sentiment, but also the notion that the bourgeoisie become the protagonists of serious

---

[2] LOUIS REYNAUD, *Le Romantisme: Les origines anglo-germaniques* (Paris: Librairie Armand Colin, 1926), p. 3.
[3] GEORGE A. AIKEN, ed., *The Tatler* (New York: Hadley & Mathews, 1899), II, 142.
[4] GREGORY SMITH, ed., *The Spectator* (London: J. M. Dent & Sons, 1963), III, 375-376.

2

dramatic action. Steele condemned the notion that tragedy deal exclusively with personages of high rank: «When unhappy catastrophes make up part of the history of princes, and persons who act in high spheres, or are represented in the moving language and well-wrought scenes of tragedians, they do not fail of striking us with terror; but then they affect us only in a transient manner, and pass through our imaginations, as incidents in which our fortunes are too humble to be concerned... Instead of such passages, I was thinking it would be of great use to lay before the world such adventures as befall persons not exalted above the common level» (*Tatler*, No. 172).[5]

The same spirit of sentimentalism which impelled Colley Cibber, Addison and Steele to new literary practices was found in the philosophic writings of Anthony Ashley Cooper, third Earl of Shaftesbury. His Treatises *An Inquiry Concerning Virtue, or Merit* (1699) and *The Moralists, a Philosophic Rhapsody* (1709) appeared together in the second volume of his *Characteristics of Men, Manners, Opinions and Times,* published in 1711.

Shaftesbury insisted upon the innate goodness of man: « 'Tis full as impossible to conceive, that a rational Creature coming first to be try'd by rational Objects, and receiving into his Mind the Images or Representations of Justice, Generosity, Gratitude, or other Virtue, shou'd have no *Liking* of these, or *Dislike* of their contrarys...»[6]

Since man's nature was good, he defended man against traditional censures, such as Hobbes and orthodox Calvinistic theology, which regarded human nature as depraved. As such Thomson called him «the friend of man» («Summer,» *Seasons,* v. 1550).[7]

Moreover, for Shaftesbury, man was in closet touch with his own nature when his emotions were freed. He drew a direct line from feeling to virtue: «And where a Series or continu'd Succession of the tender and kind Affections can be carry'd on, even thro' Fears, Horrors, Sorrows, Griefs; the Emotion of the Soul is still agreeable. We continue pleas'd even with this melancholy Aspect or Sense of Virtue... We find by our-selves, that the moving our Passions in this mournful way, the engaging them in behalf of Merit and Worth, and the exerting whatever we have of social Affection and human Sympathy, is of the highest Delight, and affords a greater Enjoyment in the way of *Thought* and *Sentiment* than any thing besides can do in a way of *Sense* and common Appetite» (II, 106-7).

Shaftesbury was a precursor of Rousseau, not only in the notion that man is basically good, but also that society makes him bad. The corruption of man's moral sense «can proceed only from the Force of Custom and Education in opposition to Nature» (II, 45).

He longed for a society in which man's emotions would lead him into an empathetic and sympathetic relationship with other men, a relationship

    [5] *The Tatler*, III, 305-306.
    [6] Earl of Shaftesbury, «An Inquiry Concerning Virtue, or Merit,» in *Characteristics of Men, Manners, Opinions and Times* (n. p., 1732), II, 43.
    [7] J. LOGIE ROBERTSON, ed., *The Complete Poetical Works of James Thomson* (London: Oxford University Press, 1908), p. 203.

18

from which all virtue flows. Since virtue is natural and vice, unnatural, virtue contains within itself its own reward, as vice does its own punishment: «For if Virtue be to it-self no small Reward, and Vice in a great measure its own Punishment; we have a solid ground to go upon.»[8]

By the third decade of the eighteenth century, sentimentalism also became the keynote in poetry and the novel. The *Seasons* (1726-1730) by James Thomson was the first considerable poem that showed Shaftesbury's influence. The moral and social value of humanitarian feelings is well exemplified in the section «Winter:»

> ...Thought fond man
> of these, and all the thousand nameless ills
> That one incessant struggle render life,
> One scene of toil, of suffering, and of fate,
> Vice in his high career would stand appalled,
> and heedless rambling Impulse learn to think;
> The conscious heart of Charity would warm,
> And her wide wish Benevolence dilate;
> The social tear would rise, the social sigh;
> And, into clear perfection, gradual bliss,
> Refining still, the social passions work. (vv. 348-358).

The new optimism of the epoch was also expressed in the *Essay on Man* (1732-34) by Alexander Pope. He proclaimed the perfection of the universe in his *Epistle* I:

> All are but parts of one stupendous whole,
> Whose body Nature is, and God the soul;
> ... ...
> As full, as perfect, in a hair as heart;
> As full, as perfect, in vile man that mourns,
> As the rapt seraph that adores and burns:
> To him no high, no low, no great, no small;
> He fills, he bounds, connects, and equals all.
>
> (I, 267-280).[9]

He insisted on happiness: «Oh happiness! our being's end and aim! / Good, pleasure, ease, content! whate'er thy name:» (*Epistle* IV, vv. 1-2), and charity:

> In faith and hope the world will disagree,
> But all mankind's concern is charity:
> All must be false that thwart this one great end;
>
> (*Epistle* III, 307-309).

two of the basic tenets of the new morality portrayed in sentimental comedy.

---

[8] «The Moralists, a Philosophic Rhapsody,» II, 275.
[9] G. B. HARRISON, ed., *Major British Writers* (New York: Harcourt, Brace and Company, 1954), p. 698.

Pope reiterated Shaftesbury's notion of the innocence and happiness of man and life in the state of nature throughout *Epistle* III:

> God in the nature of each being founds
> Its proper bliss, and sets its proper bounds:
> ... ...
> So from the first, eternal order ran,
> And creature linked to creature, man to man (vv. 109-114)
> ... ...
> Nor think, in Nature's state they blindly trod;
> The state of Nature was the reign of God:
> Self-love and social at her birth began,
> Union the bond of all things, and of man (vv. 147-150).

Society then exploits and corrupts him:

> Who first taught souls enslaved, and realms undone,
> Th'enormous faith of many made for one;
> That proud exception to all Nature's laws,
> T'invert the world, and counterwork its Cause?
> ... ...
> Zeal then, not charity, became the guide; (III, 241-244; 261).

The importance of sentimentalism and emotion can also be seen in Pope's exaltation of instinct over reason:

> Reason, however able, cool at best,
> Cares not for service, or but serves when pressed,
> Stays till we call, and then not often near;
> But honest Instinct comes a volunteer,
> Sure never to o'ershoot, but just to hit, (III, 85-89).

The English philosophic and poetic works of Locke, Shaftesbury, Pope and Thomson influenced such Spanish writers as Cadalso, Meléndez Valdés, and Jovellanos, even before making their imprint on the *comedia lacrimosa*.[10]

The eighteenth century sentimental novel, which flourished between 1750 and 1790, was also inaugurated in England by Samuel Richardson, although Jean-Jacques Rousseau wrote the most famous sentimental novel, *Julie ou La Nouvelle Héloïse* (1761), which enjoyed an enormous popularity. Richardson's three novels, *Pamela* (1740), *Clarissa Harlowe* (1747-48) and *Sir Charles Grandison* (1753-54), took the sentimental drama as their model. In these novels of great emotional intensity, sensibility and sentimentality lead to virtue. These works exemplify the philosophy of Shaftesbury con-

---

[10] For a detailed appraisal of the extent to which English philosophic works and poetry were read in Spain see Russell P. Sebold's «Enlightenment Philosophy and the Emergence of Spanish Romanticism,» in *The Ibero-American Enlightenment* (Urbana: University of Illinois Press, 1971), *Colonel Don José Cadalso* (New York: Twayne Publishers, 1971), and *El rapto de la mente:Poética y poesía dieciochescas* (Madrid: Editorial Prensa Española, 1970).

cerning both the innate goodness of man and the expression of his natural feelings as a path to virtue. This elevation of feeling supplies the persuasive element in sentimental novels and dramas and provides the basis for the conflict between the individual and social conventions. Consistent with this philosophy, the individual becomes the hero and the restraining institutions and conventions are seen as the result of prejudice and the cause of injustice. As such, Richardson's novels developed themes which became the basis of the *comedia lacrimosa*: the injustice of many laws, the abuses of parents in their relationship with their children, the theme of honor and the right of an individual to choose his own mate in opposition to *mariages de convenance.*

The middle-class is the center of concern in these novels, as it is in sentimental comedy. Perhaps Diderot, the great theorist of the *comédie larmoyante,* analyzed Richardson's novelistic innovation best: «Le monde où nous vivons [in the novels of Richardson] est le lieu de la scène; le fond de son drame est vrai; ses personnages ont toute la réalité possible; ses caractères sont pris du milieu de la société; ses incidents sont dans les moeurs de toutes les nations policées, ...les travers et les afflictions de ses personnages sont de la nature de celles qui me menacent sans cesse; il me montre le cours général des choses qui m'environnent.»[11]

His novels also adopted the didacticism, moralizing quality, and concern with feeling and emotion of sentimental drama. It is no wonder that Richardson was acclaimed by the man who was campaigning for plays with middle-class subjects; strong social and moral orientations; simple, realistic plots and touching, emotional scenes which would work on the sentiments of the audience: «O Richardson, Richardson, homme unique à mes yeux, tu seras ma lecture dans tous les temps! ... tu me resteras sur le même rayon avec Moïse, Homère, Euripide et Sophocle; et je vous lirai tour à tour. Plus on a l'âme belle, plus on a le goût exquis et pur, plus on connaît la nature, plus on aime la vérité, plus on estime les ouvrages de Richardson» («Éloge de Richardson,» p. 33).

The social evolution marked by the appearance of sentimentalism in literature was also proclaimed in painting, in which the middle-class was posed in sentimental form for didactic ends. William Hogarth was the first English artist interested in portraying the new middle-class culture. He was a·social satirist who portrayed the vices and follies of the aristocratic society of the London of his time. Works such as *A Harlot's Progress, A Rake's Progress* and the series *Mariage à la mode* (1743-45) were paintings showing moral decay.

Jean-Baptiste Simeon Chardin, a French contemporary of Hogarth, was a great critic of the immorality of French society. He painted subjects from the lower middle-class such as *Le Bénédicité, L'Ouvrière en tapisserie,* and *La Mère laborieuse,* and like Hogarth's works, these paintings had great sentimental potential.

---

[11] DENISE DIDEROT, «Éloge de Richardson,» in *Oeuvres esthétiques,* ed. Paul Vernière (Paris: Éditions Garnier-Frères, 1960), pp. 30-31.

Jean-Baptiste Greuze, a follower of Chardin, was still more emotional in his approach. Diderot extolled his paintings for their «émotion douce.» [12] He was delighted with the sentimentalities of Greuze. In his review of the *Piété filiale* he exclaimed: «Ah! mon Dieu, comme il me touche! mais si je le regarde encore, je crois que je vais pleurer... Lorsque je vis ce vieillard éloquent et pathétique, je sentis comme elle mon âme s'attendrir et des pleurs prèts à tomber de mes yeux» («Le pathétique bourgeois,» p. 525). Greuze's moralizing, anecdotic family scenes, such as *L'Accordée de village, La Malédiction paternelle,* and *Le mauvais fils puni,* were the prime source for the physical effects in domestic drama: the posturing —kneeling in petition or repentance— and the waving of anguished arms.

Diderot defended Greuze as «le premier [of our artists] qui se soit avisé, parmi nous, de donner des moeurs à l'art, et d'enchaîner des événements d'après lesquels il serait facile de faire un roman» («Le pathétique bourgeois,» p. 531).

The culmination of the sentimental vogue was found in the writings of Jean-Jacques Rousseau. Rousseau was an arch-sentimentalist. Rousseau's notions about sentiment are important in understanding the impetus behind the *comedia lacrimosa,* not merely because he sought through the exaltation of feeling suppressed instincts and repressed sentiment, but because in this liberation of the individual spirit he saw a parallel liberation of the oppressed classes. This concern for broad segments of society leads in literature to a concern for society's conduct and conventions. Artists would move towards Shelley's concept of «unacknowledged legislators of mankind.» Art became political.

Julie ou La Nouvelle Héloïse (1761) is a novel infused with sensitivity and sentiment. «Il inaugure une ère nouvelle par son culte pour l'instinct; le sentiment individuel; par la place que dans son oeuvre comme dans son âme tiennent la sensibilité, parfois maladive, l'imagination, la rêverie; par sa passion pour la nature, son ideal de vie simple, de bonté naturelle, son dédain pour les formes sociales et les contraintes traditionnelles, sa morale du coeur.» [13]

Rousseau was interested in sentiments more than ideas. His novel is a psychological analysis of souls. He composed with sensations. «L'ouvrage est moins *admiré* que profondément *senti*; ...il [Rousseau] a ému quelque fibre intime et commune plutôt qu'il n'a éveillé la délicatesse du goût ou de l'intelligence.» [14] Saint-Preux's first letter to Julie illustrates the exclamatory, sentimental style characteristic of his novel, of lachrymose drama in Spain and later Romantic plays: «Vous, me chasser! moi, vous fuir! et pourquoi? Pourquoi donc est-ce un crime d'être sensible au mérite, et d'aimer ce qu'il faut qu'on honore? Non, belle Julie; vos attraits avaient

---

[12] DENISE DIDEROT, «Le pathétique bourgeois,» in *Les Salons* of his *Oeuvres esthétiques,* p. 519.
[13] PAUL VAN TIEGHEM, *Le Romantisme dans la littérature européenne* (Paris: Éditions Albin Michel, 1948), p. 37.
[14] PHILIPPE VAN TIEGHEM, *La Nouvelle Héloïse de Jean-Jacques Rousseau* (Paris: Société Française d'Éditions Littéraires et Techniques, 1929), p. 111.

éboui mes yeux, jamais ils n'eussent égaré mon coeur sans l'attrait plus puissant qui les anime. C'est cette union touchante d'une sensibilité si vive et d'une inaltérable douceur; c'est cette pitié si tendre à tous les maux d'autrui; c'est cet esprit juste et ce goût exquis qui tirent leur pureté de celle de l'âme; ce sont, en un mot, les charmes des sentiments, bien plus que ceux de la personne, que j'adore en vous.»[15]

La Nouvelle Héloïse was a transitional work because it signified the beginning of a new reign of subjective literature: a literature of experience and confession. Like the novels of Richardson, it described events from everyday life and was didactic. Its moralizing tendency is seen throughout in its condemnation of eighteenth century French society. Rousseau called for reforms in state, church, education, family life and marriage. He wanted to discredit the institution of dueling. Julie writes a long letter to her lover about the theme of honor and dueling when she learns that he wants to avenge the insult received from milord Edouard: «...vous aggravez son outrage, vous prouvez qu'il avait raison, vous sacrifiez mon honneur à un faux point d'honneur... Cette absurdité n'a-t-elle rien qui vous révolte? Eh Dieu! quel est ce misérable honneur qui ne craint pas le vice, mais le reproche, et qui ne vous permet pas d'endurer d'un autre un démenti reçu d'avance de votre propre coeur?... Gardez-vous donc de confondre le nom sacré de l'honneur avec ce préjugé féroce qui met toutes les vertus à la pointe d'une épée» (pp. 128-130). Letter II of the Second Part condemns marriages arranged by parents without the consent of children, holding that marriage should be based upon natural feelings and affections.

One of the characteristics of Romantic literature is the interaction or rapport between man and nature. Nature becomes a confidant and is in accord with man's sentiments. This concept, while not new with Rousseau, and dating to Shaftesbury and Thomson, is fundamental in the *Nouvelle Héloïse* and will also characterize several Spanish sentimental comedies, which like nearly all Spanish Pre-Romantic and Romantic works were to some extent influenced by the Genevan philosopher and novelist.

Several of Rousseau's philosophic ideas were echoed in the *comedia lacrimosa*. Rousseau introduced a new moral system, which was in essence a reiteration of ideas already set forth by Shaftesbury and Pope. The moral criteria of society are a deformation of true virtue. All good in man comes from nature, all bad from society. Man was free and virtuous; society made him bad and miserable. He showed how the growth of civilization corrupted man's natural goodness in his *Discours sur les sciences et les arts* (1750): «nos âmes se sont corrumpües à mesure que nos Sciences et nos Arts se sont avancés à la perfection.»[16]

In the Preface to the *Discours sur l'origine de l'inégalité*, Rousseau claimed that man, by nature, is good —self sufficient, compassionate to others and from these two precepts of natural man he can establish all the

---

[15] JEAN-JACQUES ROUSSEAU, *Julie ou La Nouvelle Héloïse* (Paris: Éditions Garnier Frères, 1960), p. 6.
[16] JEAN-JACQUES ROUSSEAU, *Discours sur les sciences et les arts*, ed. George R. Havens (New York: Modern Language Association of America, 1946), p. 109.

principles of natural right: «j'y crois apercevoir deux principes antérieurs à la raison, dont l'un nous intéresse ardemment à notre bien-être et a la conservation de nous-mêmes, et l'autre nous inspire une répugnance naturelle à voir périr ou souffrir tout être sensible et principalement nos semblables. C'est du concours et de la combinaison que notre esprit est en état de faire de ces deux principes, ...que me paraissent découler toutes les règles du droit natural.»[17]

Society in order to be just must be concerned with the individual. This notion was also embraced by the Milanese jurist Cesare Beccaria in his celebrated treatise *Dei delitti e delle pene* published in 1764. According to Beccaria, laws are social in nature and the guiding principle of laws must be «la massima felicità divisa nel maggior numero.»[18] He advocated humanitarian treatment for the criminal. It is wrong to treat an accused person as though he were a criminal *a priori*: «É meglio prevenire i delitti, che punirli» (p. 88). You must prevent people going wrong beforehand: «Volete prevenire i delitti? Fate che i lumi accompagnino la libertà» (p. 89).

One of the most important results of Beccaria's treatise was that it helped put an end to torture. Beccaria raised the question: «La tortura e i tormenti sono eglino *giusti,* e ottengono eglino i *fine* che si propongono le leggi?» (p. 39). He then suggested why it should be abolished: «o il delitto è certo, o incerto; se certo, non gli conviene altra pena che la stabilità dalle leggi, ed inutile sono i tormenti, perchè inutile è la confessione del reo; se è incerto non devesi tormentare un innocente, perchè tale è secondo le leggi un uomo, i cui delitti non sono provati» (p. 45).

It was, of course, not the specific recommendations relating to the system of criminal justice in Beccaria's work that influenced the sentimental comedy in Spain but sentiment put to the use of a deep humanitarianism.

Jovellanos, the author of the best known *comedia lacrimosa, El delincuente honrado,* read Beccaria and proposed reforms of the penitentiary system and the abolition of torture. His play, as well as other lachrymose dramas in Spain, contained commentaries on the injustices and barbarities of various laws and edicts and the use of torture. Torcuato, «the honorable culprit» and protagonist of the play, condemns the use of torture to extract a confession: «La tortura!... ¡Oh nombre odioso! ¡Nombre funesto!... ¿Es posible que en un siglo en que se respeta la humanidad y en que la filosofía derrama su luz por todas partes, se escuchen aún entre nosotros los gritos de la inocencia oprimida?» (act II, scene xiv). Laura, his wife, comments on the injustice of existing judicial conditions: «... las leyes, con esas leyes bárbaras y crueles, que sólo tienen fuerza contra los desvalidos» (act V, scene v). The thesis of the play, to show the injustice of a law which inflicts capital punishment on duelists without distinguishing between the provoked and the provoker, seems to be taken directly from Beccaria: «il miglior metodo di prevenire questo delitto [dueling] è di punire l'aggresso-

---

[17] JEAN-JACQUES ROUSSEAU, *Discours sur l'origine de l'inégalité* (Paris: Garnier-Flammarion, 1971), p. 153.
[18] CESARE BECCARIA, *Dei delitti e delle pene* (Torino: Unione Tipografico-Editrice Torinese, 1911), p. 23.

re, cioè chi ha dato occasione al duello, dichiarando innocente chi senza sua colpa è stato costretto a difendere ciò che le leggi attuali non assicurano, cioè l'opinione» (*Dei delitti e delle pene*, p. 38).

Beccaria's style is also similar to what we find in sentimental comedy. His style is that of a plea to incite men to think and to act. He tells his readers: «Consultiamo il cuore umano, e in esso troveremo i principii fondamentali del vero diritto del sovrano di punire i delitti» (p. 25). Sentimental drama tries to affect man's conduct by appealing to his emotions. It aims at moral reform by an arousal of feelings and sentiment. In these dramas, as in the work of Beccaria, the pursuit of happiness is constant.

The *comedia lacrimosa* introduced a new moral code which was greatly influenced by the ideas of Rousseau and Beccaria: a new morality founded on friendship, tolerance, humanity and charity; an attack on established society and a new code of heroism. The hero in these plays is virtuous if judged from the standpoint of Rousseau—the enemy of traditional society. He is bad and Satanic if assessed by conventional social circles. The traditional outcast or pariah becomes the hero in this new age.

Rousseau set forth his ideas on drama in his *Lettre à d'Alembert sur les spectacles* (1758). He criticized comedy because it was based on ridicule. He would not pardon «le ridicule de la vertu; c'est ce qu'il a fait dans le *Misanthrope*.»[19] He continued to criticize Molière and his followers because «ce sont des gens qui, tout au plus, raillent quelquefois les vices, sans jamais faire aimer la vertu» (p. 55). On the other hand, he commended Voltaire's sentimental comedy *Nanine* because it upheld the principle of innate goodness and because in it «l'honneur, la vertu, les purs sentiments de la nature, y sont préférés à l'impertinent préjugé des conditions» (p. 36).

In spite of the fact that sentimentalism appeared in painting and all genres of literature in the eighteenth century, its main outlet was drama. Because of its dialectical nature, the theater was an excellent vehicle for the polemical and programmatical character of this new mode of expression. Sentimental comedies were first written in England just before or at the very beginning of the eighteenth century and new ones were still to appear in Spain as late as the middle of the nineteenth. To be sure, fundamental aspects of the sentimental comedy remained very much alive in the Romantic theater of all European countries.

[19] JEAN-JACQUES ROUSSEAU, *Lettre à d'Alembert sur les spectacles*, ed. L. Brunel (Paris: Librarie Hachette, 1910), p. 57.

CHAPTER II

SENTIMENTAL COMEDY:

ITS EVOLUTION IN ENGLAND AND FRANCE

It is generally agreed among critics that Colley Cibber's *Love's Last Shift, or The Fool in Fashion* (1696) was the first sentimental comedy. Ernest Bernbaum, in his excellent study on English sentimental drama, confirmed that the play «marked the beginning of a new epoch in English dramatic history.»[1] He goes on to say that Cibber «is the first dramatist to meet the demand for a sentimental representation of contemporary life» (p. 76). This play contains foreshadowings of the new tearful comedy and possesses various characteristics that were to dominate the whole course of Spanish sentimental comedy.

The play portrayed characters taken from everyday London life. One of the essential features of lachrymose comedy is the fact that ordinary middle-class citizens become the protagonists of serious and significant dramatic action. George Lillo, in the «Prologue» to his domestic tragedy *George Barnwell,* summed up this innovation:

> Forgive us, then, if we attempt to shew,
> In artless strains, a tale of private woe.
> A London 'prentice ruin'd is our theme,
> Drawn from the fam'd old song that bears his name.[2]

These bourgeois plays, also known as domestic or urban drama, *comedia urbana* or *burguesa, bürgerliches Trauerspiel,* represented a reaction against the so-called Comedy of Manners of the Restoration period, practiced by Congreve and others, which concerned itself with the manners and conventions of an artificial, highly sophisticated society.

Love's Last Shift is didactic. Another important characteristic of the sentimental comedy is its moralizing, ethical nature. It is believed that the

---

[1] ERNEST BERNBAUM, *The Drama of Sensibility: A Sketch of the History of English Sentimental Comedy and Domestic Tragedy 1696-1780* (Cambridge, Mass.: Harvard University Press, 1925), p. 9.
[2] GEORGE LILLO, «George Barnwell,» in *Modern British Drama* (London: William Miller, 1811), II, 71.

sentimental dramatists were influenced by Jeremy Collier's *A Short View of the Immorality and Profaneness of the English Stage* (1698) which was important in general in opening the way for moral reform in all literature. It charged that «the Business of *Plays* is to recommend Vertue, and discountenance Vice.»[3] He wanted to prove «the Misbehavior of the *Stage,* with respect to *Morality,* and *Religion.* Their *Liberties* in the Following Particulars are intolerable, ... Their making their top *Characters Libertines,* and giving them *Success* in their *Debauchery*» (p. 2). His influence was great in reminding dramatists that their aim should be moral.

These urban comedies portrayed a new moral code in opposition to conventional morality. Domestic drama had a close connection with the growing spirit of dissatisfaction with existing social, economic, religious and political conditions. They not only portayed middle-class life and its problems but attacked the corruption and depravity of the nobility.

They questioned the rights of the individual versus social prejudices and injustices. Now drama was concerned with the individual and the sentiments of the individual. The right of a individual to choose his own mate in marriage in opposition to conventional standards and *mariages de convenance* was to be a major and predominant theme in these plays in England, France and Spain. The new concept of morality based on friendship, tolerance, humanity and charity were principles exalted by Rousseau as fundamental to man's happiness.

At the same time, these sentimental comedies reflected the Pre-Romantic *mal du siècle* or *fastidio universal*—a general state of malaise, *taedium vital,* dissatisfaction with their destiny. «Dans ce malaise moral [in the Pre-Romantic authors] le rôle de la raison comme guide diminue; ceux de l'imagination et de la sensibilité prédominent.»[4]

One of the most prominent aspects of Cibber's *Love's Last Shift* and domestic comedy in general is its sentimentality. This genre of drama was also called sentimental, weepy, lachrymose, *lacrimoso,* because of its cultivation of sympathy, of its emphasis on sentiment, sensitivity, tenderness and its profuse emotional expression. «On y a toujours pleuré de douleur; désormais on y pleure d'attendrissement, de reconnaissance, de sympathie, de joie, ou simplement pour le plaisir de pleurer. Même quand on ne pleure pas bruyamment, on a frèquemment la larme a l'oeil, 'a starting tear!'»[5]

The nobility avoided sentimentality. The aristocratic outlook on life was reserved and self-controlled. Lachrymose comedy represented an attitude opposed to the aristocratic one. It liberated feeling and moved audiences to handkerchiefs and tears. The rationale behind the manipulative device we call sentimentalism in these plays is that with the freeing of man's spirit, the efficacy of outside force and authority in shaping his conduct would be diminished. Since sentimental drama put its faith in the innate goodness of

---

[3] JEREMY COLLIER, *A Short View of the Immorality and Profaneness of the English Stage,* 2nd ed. (1698; rpt, New York: Ams Press, 1974), p. 1.

[4] PAUL VAN TIEGHEM, *op. cit.,* p. 249.

[5] LOUIS REYNAUD, *op. cit.,* p. 56.

man, the impulse towards moral reform would now have to come from within. Feelings would now have to guide an aroused spirit to truth, happiness, and right conduct.

«The general theme [of *Love's Last Shift*], a wife's discovery of her husband's faithlessness, was commoplace. With a bold departure from convention, however, this situation was motivated and resolved on principles repugnant to the comic spirit.»[6] «What is noteworthy in the play is... the sentimentality—the characterization of Loveless as good at heart; above all, that of Amanda with her moral scrupulosity and the power of her virtue to triumph through an appeal to pity.»[7] The same theme of the unfaithful husband and the sympathetic wife was later developed by Zavala y Zamora in his *comedia lacrimosa, El bueno y el mal amigo*. Quintina plays on her husband's emotions to effect a change in his conduct. These playwrights claimed they could correct vice only by sentiment, not ridicule.

Perhaps the most innovative aspect of the sentimental comedy is that it represented a new form of tragi-comedy. It was a new genre of drama, which permitted a fusion of tragic and comic elements, and not an alternation of such elements as the Romantics would contrive later in works such as *Don Álvaro o la fuerza del sino*. The action, serious in theme, subject matter and tone, seems to be leading to a catastrophe until an unexpected turn in events brings about the happy dénouement.

By increasing the emotional element in comedy, comedy comes into closer relationship with tragedy. In pure comedy, emotion, especially sentimentality, is avoided. The opposite is true in tragedy. According to Aristotle, the purpose of tragedy was to arouse the emotions of pity and fear and thus to produce in the audience a catharsis of these emotions.

Eighteenth century critics argued as to whether sentimental comedy represented a new dramatic genre or a renovation of classical models by authors such as Euripides, Menander, Plautus and especially Terence. Steele was the first writer to interpret Terence as a model for sentimental dramatists: «There are in the Play of the *Self-Tormentor [Hauton Timorumenos]* of Terence's which is allowed a most excellent Comedy, several Incidents which would draw Tears from any Man of Sense, and not one which would move his Laughter.»[8]

Diderot also defended Terence and his bourgeois drama *Hecyra* as precedents for the drama of sensibility: «Toutes les comédies de Térence furent applaudies. L'*Hécyre* seule, composée dans un genre particulier, eut moins de succès que les autres: le poète en avait banni le personnage plaisant. En se proposant d'introduire le goût d'une comédie tout à fait grave et sérieuse, il ne comprit pas que cette composition dramatique ne souffre pas une scène faible, et que la force de l'action et du dialogue doit remplacer partout la gaieté des personnages subalternes.»[9] *Hecyra* is an example of what Diderot called *le genre sérieux*: «Je demande dans quel genre est cette

---

[6] ERNEST BERNBAUM, *op. cit.*, p. 72.
[7] *Ibid.*, p. 76.
[8] *The Spectator*, No. 521 (Postscript to No. 502), IV, 145.
[9] DENISE DIDEROT, «Éloge de Térence,» in *Oeuvres esthétiques*, pp. 58-59.

pièce? Dans le genre comique? Il n'y a pas le mot pour rire. Dans le genre tragique? La terreur, la commisération et les autres grandes passions n'y sont excitées... J'appellerai ce genre le *genre sérieux*.»[10]

On the other hand, Oliver Goldsmith could not really claim Terence as a model: «Since the first origin of the Stage, Tragedy and Comedy have run in distinct channels and never till of late encroached upon the provinces of each other. Terence seems to have made the nearest approaches, yet always judiciously stops short before he comes to downright pathetic.»[11]

Euripides' tragedies had an air of melodrama, and the bourgeois tone of his heroes was frequent. He introduced characters and problems from contemporary life such as arranging suitable marriages. The so—called bourgeois «New Comedy» of Menander was often sentimental, moving and very moralizing. «Perhaps [a] greater obstacle to our appreciation [of Menander's plays] is their traditional classification as comedies. It is true that the sequence of highly improbable coincidences prevents our taking the plot seriously, that the exalted personages of tragedy have given way to commonplace types with names as transparent as Squire Allworthy's, that these characters are concerned, not with large problems of destiny, but with family matters... But these are serious dramas.»[12] Plautus' comedy *Captivi* «engages the emotions of the reader as no other ancient comedy does.»[13] *Trinummus* is noteworthy for its realism and ethical character. Terence's *Andria* has often been called a sentimental comedy. Pamphilus is in love with a supposed orphan Glycerium, but his father has already arranged for his marriage to the daughter of Chremes, Philumena. Glycerium also turns out to be Chremes' daughter and in the end Pamphilus marries her. The play, because of its subject matter—the right to choose one's partner in marriage; the theme of recognition which brings about a change of fortune from bad to good; and the predominant emotional tone, is an excellent prototype for the sentimental comedy.

Nevertheless, while the Greeks and Romans furnished precedents for sentimental drama by placing serious elements in comedy, bourgeois ones in tragedy, the genre *per se* never experienced a life of its own until the eighteenth century.

In order to understand the principles which lie behind this new genre of tragi-comedy, sentimental drama must be examined in relation to the classic notions of comedy and tragedy. According to Aristotle, comedy is «an imitation of characters of a lower type» (*Poetics*, V, 1).[14] Sentimental comedy also deals with the problems of men and women of the middle and lower classes.

[10] DENISE DIDEROT, «Entretiens sur le fils naturel,» *Oeuvres esthétiques*, p. 136.

[11] OLIVER GOLDSMITH, «An Essay on the Theatre; or, A Comparison between Laughing and Sentimental Comedy,» in *Collected Works of Oliver Goldsmith*, ed. Arthur Friedman (Oxford: Oxford University Press, 1966), III, 211.

[12] MOSES HADAS, *A History of Greek Literature* (New York: Columbia University Press, 1950), pp. 191-192.

[13] MOSES HADAS, *A History of Latin Literature* (New York: Columbia University Press, 1952), p. 38.

[14] S. H. BUTCHER, ed. and trans., *Aristotle's Theory of Poetry and Fine Art* (New York: Dover Publications, 1951), p. 21.

One of the essential elements of comedy is ridicule. Since comedy ridicules the frailties of man, it professes a moral aim. Aristophanes, the great Greek dramatist of «Old Comedy,» insisted upon the didactic and moral as well as the pleasurable goals of comedy. In several passages in *Acharnians* and *Frogs* he claims that the function of the comic playwright is to instruct and guide: «For boys a teacher at school is found, but we, the poets, / are teachers of men. / We are bound things honest and pure to speak/» (*Frogs,* vv. 1054-1056).[15] Because it has a different attitude towards the class it treats than classical comedy, sentimental drama never uses the tool of ridicule. It substitutes emotion for ridicule. Sentimental dramatists insist that comedy should have a higher purpose than merely to ridicule the weaknesses of mankind.

Aristotle never explicitly assigned comedy an inferior role to that of tragedy. Nevertheless, based on the distinctions he made between musical forms in *Politics,* he probably found comedy lacking the seriousness needed to attain the highest ideals of art. Molière insisted that comedy aims primarily at amusement. Boileau, in his definition of comedy in *L'Art poétique* (1674), said: «Le comique ennemi des soupirs et des pleurs, / N'admet point en ses vers de tragiques douleurs/» (Chant III; vv. 401-402).[16] Sentimental comedy, on the other hand, does not aim to amuse. It wants the audience to experience pity for the character's distresses and admiration for his virtues. Sad, moving scenes are an essential part of lachrymose drama.

In both, the dénoument is double in its issue. Virtue is rewarded and vice punished. This principle of «poetic justice» is illustrated in many sentimental comedies.

Sentimental comedy possesses several characteristics that are incompatible with the classic concept of tragedy and the tragic hero. Oliver Goldsmith referred to this genre as «bastard tragedy.»[17]

According to the classic definition of tragedy, the protagonist must be a person of distinction, of high rank. He possesess *grandeur,* valor and courage. The Greek tragedians' emphasis was on the capacity of great figures to adapt themselves to the trials of life. While the common man's afflictions might be considered pathetic, they were not tragic. Running contrary to this concept, sentimental drama refuses to believe that virtuous and heroic persons cannot be found in the sphere of the middle-class. The middle-class citizen becomes the hero. Sentimental drama attempts, through the representation of bourgeois situations, to make the emotional force of tragedy more widely effective.

Bourgeois tragedy properly belongs to an age of science. Man, who was viewed in classical tragedy as alone, independent and, most importantly, responsible for his actions and their consequences, is now, on the other hand, seen as a product of his environment which is no longer merely a

---

[15] ANDREW CHIAPPE, ed., Benjamin Bickley Rogers, trans., *Five Comedies of Aristophanes* (New York: Doubleday & Co., 1955), p. 123.

[16] NICHOLAS BOILEAU-DESPRÉAUX, *Épitres, Art poétique, Lutrin* (Paris: Société les belles lettres, 1939), p. 108.

[17] OLIVER GOLDSMITH, *op. cit.,* p. 212.

setting for action but becomes an active element in determining that action. With this deterministic view man's responsibility is diminished.

In tragedy «a well constructed plot should be single in its issue, rather than double as some maintain. The change of fortune should be not from bad to good, but, reversely, from good to bad» (*Poetics*, XIII, 4). The change from adversity to prosperity, according to Aristotle, fails to produce the proper tragic effect. Sentimental drama, as noted previously, is double in its issue with punishment or misfortune for the wicked, and reward or prosperity for the good. If the evil characters are not punished *per se* they admit their guilt and often beg forgiveness. The change of fortune is practically always from bad to good, but while the dénouement is happy, this does not occur until the very last moment.

Of the twenty-seven *comedias lacrimosas* under consideration in this book only one, *Las víctimas del amor, Ana y Sindhám,* by Zavala y Zamora, ends on a somber, gloomy note. In all of the others we see a reflection of Shaftesbury's beliefs, as the struggle of virtue against distress is finally rewarded by happiness. «The spectacle of virtue always triumphant [to the Greek tragedians] could only corroborate smugness; the spectacle of flawless virtue crushed to earth would only be shocking, as Aristotle points out. If in the elemental struggle against destiny man seems doomed to defeat, that is the way life looked to the tragedians.»[18]

The powers which defeat the protagonist in classical tragedy must be overwhelming, awe-inspiring. The effect of the action upon the audience is to produce pity and fear. In sentimental comedy we are no longer dealing with overwhelming powers but rather social injustices, unhappy marriages, domineering and dictatorial parents, cruel and harsh laws which oppress the protagonist. The character's conduct is so presented as to arouse pity for his sufferings.

Tragedy is based on a well-known legend. The audience does not concentrate on the outcome of the story, but rather «on the way in which he [the hero] responds to the challenge which confronts him, on his daring, or on his ability to bear the worst that heaven and earth can devise. The focus is thus upon his grandness rather than his goodness.»[19] The themes of sentimental comedy, which are taken from real life situations, are not known beforehand. Indeed the curiosity of the audience is held in suspense until the very end. This element of mystery will also be characteristic of Romantic drama.

Tragedy as defined in Aristotle's *Poetics* had nothing whatever to do with the arousal of emotions to instruct or guide man's life. For Aristotle, the evocation of pity and fear served to bring man to a state of tragic pleasure, a state of acceptance. It was the peculiar province of bourgeois tragedy to use emotion, not to effect an experience within the theater, but actions outside of it.

In spite of the distinctions, the lachrymose comedy does inherit certain

---

[18] MOSES HADAS, *A History of Greek Literature,* p. 75.
[19] ALEXANDER PREMINGER, ed., *Encyclopedia of Poetry and Poetics* (Princeton: Princeton University Press, 1965), p. 861.

characteristics directly from tragedy. One of the most recognizable traits of this genre is the theme of recognition: «a change from ignorance to knowledge, producing love or hate between the persons destined by the poet for good or bad fortune» (*Poetics*, XI, 2). «This recognition... will produce either pity or fear; and actions producing these effects are those which, by our definition, Tragedy represents. Moreover, it is upon such situations that the issues of good or bad fortune will depend» (*Poetics*, XI, 4). Aristotle speaks highly of this device as an inexhaustible source of dramatic emotion. «Roman comedy... is composed of... improbable coincidences and recognitions of long-lost daughters, irate fathers, and impertinent slaves... Separations of families, loss and even ultimate recovery of identity, and surely seduction must actually have been common during the wars and unsettled conditions of the early Hellenistic age.»[20]

As Hadas points out, themes of separation, discovery and recognition were appropriate to classical tragedy because they paralleled contemporary experience. Their use many centuries later in sentimental comedy or bourgeois tragedy was purely artificial. They were a device to arouse emotions. Although the theme of recognition was present in earlier sentimental comedies, it was not prominent until Steele's *The Conscious Lovers* (1722). After that date it became a frequent and almost constant attribute of the genre in all countries. It was also frequently found is Spanish Romantic dramas of the nineteenth century, such as *La conjuración de Venecia*, *Alfredo*, *El paje*, *Don Álvaro*, *Doña Mencía* and *Simón Bocanegra*.

Implied behind the device of recognition is the belief that life holds more in store for us than the surface of reality would indicate. What is implied behind a child borne in a manger or one fetched out of a swamp is that true and essential nobility rests outside recognizable forms, and as such its potential is in all mankind. This, of course, is Rousseau's concept of negative education and innocence thriving in the state of nature.

In Aristotle's definition, «embellished language» (*Poetics*, VI, 2) is included among the constituent elements of tragedy. Horace also speaks of language of a texture strong and bold: «Aeschylus et modicis instravit pulpita tignis, / Et docuit magnumque loqui nitique cothurno» (*Ars Poetica* I, 15).[21] Sentimental drama contains the same impassioned, eloquent and sublime language as classical tragedy.

While classic and neo-classic tragedy were written in verse, sentimental drama was often written in prose. George Lillo's domestic tragedy, *The London Merchant* (1731) introduced this innovation. While earlier sentimental comedies and domestic tragedies contained some particularly moving scenes written in prose, this play was the first to use prose throughout. The initial example of *bürgerliches Trauerspiel*, Lessing's *Miss Sara Sampson* (1755), was written in prose. Diderot, in his dramatic essay *De la poésie dramatique* (1758) recommended the use of prose, not verse, as the more

---

[20] MOSES HADAS, *A History of Latin Literature*, p. 34.
[21] J.-C. BARBIER, *Les deux arts poétiques d'Horace et de Boileau*, ed., Ernest Thorin (Paris: Librairie du Collège de France et de l'École Normale Supérieure, 1874), p. 38.

natural vehicle for domestic drama: «Je me suis demandé quelquefois si la tragédie domestique se pouvait écrire en vers; et, sans trop savoir pourquoi, je me suis répondu que non. Cependant, la comédie ordinaire s'écrit en vers; la tragédie héroïque s'écrit en vers.»[22] He wanted to replace the stiff, stilted alexandrine with the natural diction of everyday. Both of his *comédies larmoyantes* were written in prose, as was Sedaine's *Le Philosophe sans le savoir*.

Only four of the twenty-seven Spanish lachrymose comedies treated in this book were written in prose: *El delincuente honrado, Eduardo y Federica* and *El triunfo del amor y la amistad, Jenwal y Faustina* by Zavala y Zamora and *El precipitado* by Trigueros. In the «Advertencia del impresor» that precedes *El precipitado* the publisher indicates that Trigueros wrote in prose because «le parece que la naturalidad, que huie del verso, i de la compresión, habita en la prosa... Como es tan notoria la facultad que el Autor tiene para la versificación, nadie sospechará que el usar de la prosa en esta, i en otras comedias, lo hizo por impotencia.» The more prevalent use of verse in the *comedia lacrimosa* of Spain is a concession to Spanish taste.

Nevertheless, the innovation of prose as the medium of drama was of great importance in Spain also, for it continues to be used there in the offspring of sentimental comedy: nineteenth century Romantic drama, with the peculiar feature that in many Spanish examples of the latter genre it alternates with verse.

While Cibber, Farquhar and Estcourt wrote sentimental comedies, it was not until Richard Steele's plays appeared that we had examples of the fully developed type. *The Conscious Lovers* (1722) presented the theme of choosing one's mate. The hero must renounce Indiana, whom he loves, to please his parents. The play is constructed in such a way as to keep the audience in suspense until the very end. It introduces the theme of recognition—Indiana's recovery of her parent. The main characters are virtuous people, contending with afflictions throughout the play, but finally rewarded with happiness.

The most famous English sentimental dramas, and the ones most frequently imitated by the Spanish playwrights, were *The London Merchant* (1731) and *The Gamester* (1753) by Edward Moore.

Lillo's *The London Merchant* appeared under various titles: *The Merchant, The History of George Barnwell, George Barnwell*. It was an important model because of its bourgeois environment with discussions about commerce and trade; its new concept of morality—the hero, a merchant's clerk is both Satanic (misguided by his mistress Millwood, the villain of the play, he embezzles money and murders his uncle) and virtuous (his friend Trueman and his employer's daughter, Maria, are convinced of the goodness of his heart); the theme of friendship, exemplified in Trueman, the faithful, devoted friend; the lugubrious and somber tone—the farewell scenes with bells tolling and tears flowing as George Barnwell is about to be executed;[23]

---

[22]   DENISE DIDEROT, «De la poésie dramatique,» in *Oeuvres esthétiques*, p. 216.
[23]   The supposition can be made that the farewell scenes of *The London Merchant* influenced Jovellanos' execution scene of *El delincuente honrado*.

3

the use of prose and the natural language of everyday. Valladares de Soto-mayor's *El fabricante de paños, o El comerciante inglés* and Zavala y Za-mora's *El triunfo del amor, Jenwal y Faustina* were based upon this play.

The Gamester also ended tragically when Beverly, a gambler, falsely accused of murder, committed suicide by taking poison. He died just after hearing that a large amount of money had been left to him. The play also incorporated the middle-class ambiance, sentimentality, the new moral code and use of prose found in *The London Merchant*. We feel sympathy for the hero who is led astray under the influence of his false friend.

Leonardo, in Zavala y Zamora's *El bueno y el mal amigo* was probably modeled after Beverly. He is an unfaithful husband who spends his days gambling and drinking in the cafés of Madrid. Leonardo is influenced by two friends, the charitable and virtuous Anselmo and the treacherous Clau-dino. Even though Leonardo is an unfit father and husband he is generally good of heart.

Sentimental comedy was popular in England through the early 1770's. The French *comédie larmoyante* was a direct descendent of English domestic drama. Philippe Néricault Destouches, a comic dramatist of the school of Molière, spent several years in England and had contact with English senti-mental comedy. His play, *Le Philosophe marié* (1727), the first French drama that showed characteristics of lachrymose comedy, was written in England. He introduced feeling, compassion and pity to compensate for the loss of the comic element. The play was also noteworthy for its virtuous characters, its moralizing quality and the theme of recognition.

Destouches' *Le Glorieux* (1732) contained a preface which was a de-claration of the author's intention: «J'ai toujours eu pour maxime incon-testable, que quelque amusante qui puisse être une Comédie, c'est un ouvra-ge imparfait et même dangereux, si l'Auteur ne s'y propose pas de corriger les moeurs, de tomber sur le ridicule, de décrier le vice, et de mettre la vertu dans un si beau jour, qu'elle s'attire l'estime et la vénération pu-blique.»[24] Destouches was the immediate precursor of La Chaussée.

And Nivelle de la Chaussée is generally considered the inventor of the *comédie larmoyante* because «il en fit l'essence et y fonda le mérite de son drame... Il donna vraiment l'existence au genre larmoyant en lui donnant l'indépendance.»[25] His first play, *La Fausse antipathie*, appeared in 1733. His two greatest successes were *Le Préjugé à la mode* (1735), translated by Luzán into Spanish in 1751, with the title *La razón contra la moda*, and *Mélanide* (1741). The comic element was completely eliminated in the latter play. The importance of featuring an unimportant name in the title is a significant symbol of the fact that the ordinary human being is now the subject of tragedy. This would also be a pattern in the *comedia lacri-mosa*: *Eduardo y Federica, La Cecilia, Cecilia, viuda, Rufino y Aniceta, Las víctimas del amor; Ana y Sindhám, El triunfo del amor y la amistad,*

[24] *Les oeuvres de théâtre de Mr. Néricault Destouches* (Paris: François le Breton, 1716), II, n.p. (Preface).
[25] GUSTAVE LANSON, *Nivelle de la Chaussée et la comédie larmoyante*, 2nd ed. (1903; rpt. Geneva: Slatkine Reprints, 1970), p. 45.

Jenwal y Faustina, La Adelina, Natalia y Carolina and *Cecilia, la cieguecita.*

Many characteristics of La Chaussée's *comédies* reappeared in Spanish sentimental comedy. The dramas dealt with some somber aspect of domestic life. The most common theme was the desire and right of lovers to choose their own mates in opposition to the prejudices of their parents and others. As noted before, this was the most common theme in Spanish lachrymose comedy. The abuse of authority in the parent-child relationship was another prominent theme. *Comedias lacrimosas* such as *El hijo reconocido* and *Natalia y Carolina* by Luciano Francisco Comella, *El amor dichoso* and *Eduardo y Federica* by Zavala y Zamora also portrayed this theme.

La Chaussée's plays were constructed in such a way as to keep the audience constantly in suspense and to prevent their knowing the fate of the characters until the very end. Scenes of recognition were frequent. This too was characteristic of Spanish domestic comedy [26] and later Romantic drama.

Because of La Chaussée's moralizing intent, his characters are often excessively good or bad. This melodramatic note, frequently a feature in Spanish lachrymose comedy, is exemplified in the already cited play of Zavala y Zamora, *El bueno y el mal amigo.* It is difficult to believe that Quintina can so easily forgive a husband who has repeatedly hurt her so much. It is equally astonishing that Leonardo's dear friend Anselmo would continue to help him when he constantly breaks his promises to change, repent and mend his ways. Claudino, on the other hand is a miserable, conniving person who continually exerts his poor influence on Leonardo. He never hesitates to ask Leonardo for favors but is never willing to help his «friend» in times of difficulty. Cecilia, in Comella's *Cecilia, viuda* is so virtuous that she will not even tell the judge of Nicasio's evil ways towards her. She forgives and pardons all those who have dealt treacherously with her.

One of the keynotes of La Chaussée's theater is its sensibility. The themes of friendship, love, pity, charity and beneficence are important. The pursuit of happiness is constant. The characters are *sensibles,* virtuous and by nature good. Social institutions and social prejudices lead them astray. In the course of the play there is a great opportunity for the shedding of tears. Mélanide cried in a desert for seventeen years and cries incessantly throughout the five acts of the play.

His literary style is representative of this highly charged emotional tone. This style, characterized by broken phrases, exclamation points, ideas stated in an indirect, abstract, roundabout manner, will also be characteristic of Spanish sentimental comedy and Romantic drama.

If Nivelle de la Chaussée was the great playwright of sentimental comedy, then Denise Diderot was the great theorist. He wanted to renovate theater. According to him, comedy and tragedy no longer held the interest of a modern viewer, because they were too removed from reality. A new

---

[26] See, for example, *El vinatero de Madrid, Las vivanderas ilustres, El precipitado, El delincuente honrado.*

dramatic formula, which mingled tragic and comic elements and was capable of moving the audience, had to be created. «L' art doit émouvoir.» In the third of his *Entretiens sur «Le Fils naturel»* he declared his desire for a new genre: «le genre sérieux... Le genre sérieux... est... le moins sujet aux vicissitudes des temps et des lieux... Si vous excellez dans le genre sérieux, vous plairez dans tous les temps et chez tous les peuples.»[27]

His dramatic theories were developed in two essays which accompanied his two original *comédies larmoyantes.* His ideas became the basic tenets of the Spanish *comedia lacrimosa.* In the first of these essays, *Entretiens sur «Le Fils naturel»* (1757) Diderot insisted on the following: «Que le sujet en soit important; et l'intrigue, simple, domestique, et voisine de la vie réelle» (3rd. *Entretien,* p. 139). Diderot wanted dramatists to deal with social issues and conventions in plays with simple arguments.

Many *comedias lacrimosas* offer social critiques: Patricio, in Zavala y Zamora's *El amor perseguido y la virtud triunfante* says «Y finalmente, es la Corte / una habitación continua / de la confusión, el luxo, / la profusión, y la envidia» (act III). Doña Francisca, in Comella's *El hijo reconocido* notes that this is an age when they promise everything but give nothing: «no hay más que toma de industria / y daca el comercio: ciencias / por arriba, economía / por abaxo, mucha idea, / mucho plan, mucho proyecto, / si señor, grandes arengas / y al fin paja» (act I). *La Cecilia* and *Las vivanderas ilustres,* to name only two plays, contain attacks on the nobility and their corruption. *Cecilia, viuda* attacks despotism in the government. Frequently one finds a praise of work, its identification with honor and virtue and an attack on the unproductive aristocracy. Luis, a young lad in *Cecilia, viuda* declares: «Más honrado es quien gana / el pan sudando / que el honrado que vive / del ocio esclavo» (act II). Juan, the wine merchant in *El vinatero de Madrid,* makes a similar declaration: «Mira, quando cuesta el pan / más sudor, luego al comerlo / es más delicado, más / dulce, y hace más provechoso» (act I). *El abuelo y la nieta* critizices existing religious conditions, especially the role of the *abate.* Other serious themes include discussions of trade, commerce and financial matters *(El amante generoso, El fabricante de paño);* education *(La buena nuera);* the unfaithful husband and virtuous wife *(El bueno y el mal amigo);* commentaires on rigid laws on dueling *(El delincuente honrado),* and incest *(El precipitado)* and, of course, the theme of choosing one's mate—a topic of discussion in practically all of the plays. The settings are filled with details from everyday life whether it be social types, food, dress, speech, institutions or customs. The plots are simple in their construction, generally presenting a single action. If a subordinate one exists, it is important in its relation to the main plot.

Diderot wanted the action to be executed exclusively by the main characters: «Je n'y veux point de valets... point de personnages épisodiques» (3rd. *Entretien,* p. 139). Spanish sentimental comedies usually contain five or six characters with no maids or valents.

---

[27] DENISE DIDEROT, «Entretiens sur le fils naturel,» *Oeuvres esthétiques,* p. 138.

Diderot favoured visual and sensual effects which would stimulate the sensibility of the audience. «Il faut s'occuper fortement de la pantomime... et trouver des tableaux» (3rd. *Entretien,* p. 139). «J'aimerais bien mieux des tableaux sur la scène... [que] produiraient un effect si agréable..., que ces coups de théâtre» (1st *Entretien,* p. 88). Diderot elaborated on the art of pantomime in his other dramatic essay *De la poésie dramatique* (1758).

All the *comedias lacrimosas* contain actions which lead to a series of optically impressive «tableaux.» These are moving scenes à la Greuze, produced by the posturing and gesturing of the actors. Some particularly noteworthy «tableaux» include: *El fabricante de paños o El comerciante inglés,* when the cloth-merchant's workmen walk across the stage as the bailiffs arrive: «Los seis oficiales de Vilson, salen por la puerta del almacén con delantales, y cruzan la scena para ir a la tienda, caminando lentamente los brazos caídos, las cabezas vajas, y en una profunda tristeza» (act II); *El precipitado:* «Don Amato sale precipitadamente, i se arroja llorando a los pies de su padre; el padre le levanta enternecido, i le abraza» (act III, scene viii); and *El vinatero de Madrid:* «Sale Angelita; y viendo a su Padre, se precipita en sus brazos, y le conduce á los pies de Don Justo, donde ella se arrodilla llorando» (act II).

The use of pantomime, found in minute stage directions, is also fundamental in Spanish domestic comedy: *El precipitado:* «Cándida lee para sí, se turba, i suspira disimuladamente: ya mira al Cielo, ya a Doña Gracia: al fin se serena» (act I, scene i); *El amor dichoso:* «Belisa, como volviendo de un letargo, reconoce á Danteo, y enagenada del gozo, da un grito descompasado, y cae trastornada en los brazos de Danteo» (act II).

Diderot wanted plays with a strong moral thrust: «Que votre morale soit générale et forte» (3rd. *Entretien,* p. 139). All *comedias lacrimosas* follow this dogma. Many treat the theme of suicide: *(El amante generoso, La buena nuera, Cecilia, la cieguecita, El amor dichoso);* others the subject of honor *(El amante honrado, La Cecilia, Eduardo y Federica);* fortune *(El trapero de Madrid, El fabricante de paños);* dueling *(El delincuente honrado, Rufino y Aniceta, El amante generoso);* and the topic of dignity *(Las vivanderas ilustres, El bueno y el mal amigo).*

In place of the characters of classical theater, who were used as representatives of a class, Diderot wished to substitute individuals shaped by elements of their environment, such as their work and family relations: «Que ce ne sont plus... les caractères qu'il faut mettre sur la scène, mais les conditions... Il faut que la condition devienne aujourd'hui l'objet principal, et que le caractère ne soit que l'accessoire... C'est la condition, ses devoirs, ses avantages, ses embarras, qui doivent servir de base à l'ouvrage» (3rd. *Entretien,* p. 153). The drama would be based on profession: «l'homme de lettres, le philosophe, le commerçant, le juge, l'avocat, le politique, le citoyen, le magistrat, le financier, le grand seigneur, l'intendant» and family: «le père de famille, l'époux, la soeur, les frères» (3rd. *Entretien,* p. 154).

The *comedia lacrimosa* portrays characters within the confines of familial, professional, and commercial relationships. These are people modified by the circumstances of their existence. Valladares de Sotomayor wrote bour-

geois comedies with prudent merchants as protagonists: the rag dealer in
El trapero de Madrid, the cloth-merchant in *El fabricante de paños,* the
coal merchant in *El carbonero de Londres* and the wine merchant in *El vinatero de Madrid. La buena nuera* presents a mayor, usurer, scribe and
pawn-broker. *Las vivanderas ilustres* describes the wretched life of two
sutlers and the humiliation one of them, Gertrudis, must suffer at the
hands of the colonel. *El delincuente honrado* portrays the agonies of an
accused man vis à vis two judges, one conservative and the other humane
and enlightened. The role of the devoted, virtuous friend is important in
this play, as well as in many other *comedias lacrimosas.*

Most Spanish urban dramas are based on family. Mothers are usually
lacking in these plays. The most frequent combinations are husband-wife,
father-son, father-daughter, uncle-nephew, uncle-niece, and brother-sister.
Rarer are the concurrence of brother-brother, cousin-cousin, grandfather-
grandson or granddaughter, father-in-law-daughter-in-law, aunt-niece and
mother-daughter.

Diderot insisted on the use of tears to present the moral. All the Spanish
plays of this genre are highly charged emotionally and tears flow freely.

The dramatic theories of Diderot were illustrated in the two *comédies
larmoyantes* he wrote, both in five acts and in prose.

Le Fils naturel ou Les épreuves de la vertu, (1757) portrays the agonies
of Dorval, a young, tender, virtuous man who is a victim of prejudice
because of his illegitimate birth. He speaks of his problem to Constance, a
young widow and sister of his friend Clairville: «Je suis... sombre et
mélancolique. J'ai... de la vertu, mais elle est austère...» (act IV, scene
iii).[28] «Abandonné presque en naissance entre le désert et la société, quand
j'ouvris les yeux afin de reconnaitre les liens qui pouvaient m'attacher aux
hommes, à peine en trouvai-je des débris. Il y avait trente ans, madame,
que j'errais parmi eux, isolé, inconnu, négligé, sans avoir éprouvé la ten-
dresse de personne, ni rencontré personne qui recherchât la mienne, lorsque
votre frère vint à moi» (act IV, scene iii). Dorval is in love with his best
friend's sweetheart, named Rosalie. Great issues of conscience are thrashed
out in impassioned, eloquent language. To respect the obligations of friendship he decides to overcome his passion: «Vertu! douce et cruelle idée!...
Amitié qui m'enchaîne et me déchire, vous serez obéie!... Amitié, tu n'es
qu'un vain nom, si tu n'imposes aucune loi... Clairville épousera donc
Rosalie» (act III, scene ix). At the end of the play, in a moving scene of
recognition, Lysimond, father of Rosalie, returns and declares that Dorval
is his son. Clairville will marry Rosalie and Dorval, Constance.

The play served as an important model for major aspects of many *comedias lacrimosas:* the theme of the hero's view of himself as abandoned, alone,
an outcast and victim of a hostile fate;[29] the theme of friendship; the peculiar

[28] DENISE DIDEROT, «Le Fils naturel,» in *Oeuvres complètes,* ed. J. Assezat (Paris:
Garnier Frères, 1875), VII, 64.

[29] Consider Dorval's words in act IV, scene iii: «Quand je pense que nous sommes
jetés, tout en naissant, dans un chaos de préjugés, d'extravagances, de vices et de
misères, l'idée m'en fait frémir.» «...Le malheur me suit et se répand sur tout ce qui

twist of two friends in love with the same girl, found in Comella's *Los dos amigos;* the scene of recognition which converts the lugubrious trend of the play into a happy dénouement; and the sentimental, emotional tone throughout («il soupire profondément,» «des larmes tombaient de ses yeux,» «Rosalie pleure amèrement»).

Le Père de famille (1758) took up the theme (already popular in sentimental comedy) of choosing one's mate. M. D'Orbesson, «le père de famille,» has two children, Cécile and Saint-Albin, each of whom loves someone of a lower social class. Saint-Albin tells his father of his love for Sophie: «Elle est pauvre, elle est ignorée; elle habite un réduit obscur. Mais c'est un ange» (act I, scene vii).[30] M. D'Orbesson, aided in his prejudices by the opinions of his brother-in-law, opposes these unions:

SAINT-ALBIN:

Elle [Sophie] est belle, elle est sage!... Quelle est donc la femme qui me convient?

LE PÈRE:

Celle qui, par son éducation, sa naissance, son état et sa fortune, peut assurer votre bonheur et satisfaire à mes espérances.

SAINT-ALBIN:

Ainsi le mariage sera pour moi un lien d'intérêt et d'ambition!... Il me faut une compagne honnête et sensible, qui m'apprenne à supporter les peines de la vie, et non une femme riche et titrée qui les accroisse (act II, scene vi).

These attitudes of M. D'Orbesson cause the son to rebel: «L'autorité! Ils n'ont que ce mot... Des pères! des pères! il n'y en a point... Il n'y a que des tyrans» (act II, scene vi). When Sophie turns out to be the brother-in-law's niece, the father decides to bless, in the midst of high-wrought ecstasies of emotion, the marriage of his two children.

There is hardly a *comedia lacrimosa* which does not take up this theme. Zavala y Zamora's *Las víctimas del amor: Ana y Sindhám* is a good example. Ana, daughter of a Lord, is secretly married to Sindhám, a servant of the same Lord. They must hide the fact that they are married because of their different social classes, in spite of the sincerity of their feelings for one another. Milor Darambi, a tough, unsympathetic man, does not care what his daughter will think of the marriage he has arranged for her to the Baron de Fronsvill. The Baron, on the other hand, is a compassionate and understanding person who does not want to marry Ana against her will: «Mas antes / la casara yo, os confieso, / con un pobre virtuoso / que con un rico soberbio» (act I). Milor Darambi's change of heart comes too late; Sindhám dies and then Ana dies of a broken heart. The theme of domineering

m'approche... J'ai senti dans mon coeur que l'univers ne serait jamais pour moi qu'une vaste solitude sans une compagne qui partageât mon bonheur et ma peine...» (act IV, scene i).
  [30] DENISE DIDEROT, «Le Père de famille,» in *Oeuvres complètes,* ed. J. Assezat (Paris: Garnier Frères, 1875), VII, 197.

and dictatorial parents, seen in *Le Père de famille,* is also taken up in this *comedia lacrimosa.*

The most important discipline of the new theories of La Chaussée and Diderot was Michel-Jean Sedaine. *Le Philosophe sans le savoir* (1765) was the only play he wrote in this genre, but it was considered one of the masterpieces of the *comédie larmoyante.*

The play reflected the growing importance of commerce and the emerging middle-class in the eighteenth century. The protagonist, M. Vanderk *père,* of noble descent, is an honest, prudent merchant who views labor and trade as basic and important elements of the society in which he lives. «Le philosophe» exemplifies all the virtues of a good citizen, father and husband. He is a sensitive and beneficent man. His son, M. Vanderk *fils,* retains the prejudice of the nobility against commerce. Valladares de Sotomayor was obviously influenced by the spirit of this play. Four of his domestic dramas have heroes who are prudent merchants and contain discussions about trade and commerce.

Le Philosophe sans le savoir is also a satire on the pride and depravity of the nobility. The Marchioness, sister of M. Vanderk *père,* is the very embodiment of the pretentiousness and narrow prejudices of this class: «Vous, mon frère, vous avez perdu toute idée de noblesse et de grandeur; le commerce rétrécit l'âme, mon frère» (act IV, scene v).[31] This, too, was a common theme in Spanish sentimental comedy. Juan, a poor wine merchant in *El vinatero de Madrid,* commenting on the Marquis' going back on his word to marry his daughter says: «De qué sirve la nobleza / sin buenos procedimientos? / Si á la virtud no conoce, / y la persigue, es lo mesmo / que un sol eclipsado, pues / pierde así su lucimiento» (act I). The mayor makes a similar criticism in Act II of the same play: «Pero ser noble, / y proceder mal, yo creo / que es mala nobleza.» Comella's *La Cecilia* and *Cecilia viuda* are filled with comments criticizing the deceptions and cunning of the aristocrat who continually places satisfaction of desires above moral law.

Sedaine wanted to criticize the code of honor and censure the savage institution of dueling. In Act III M. Vanderk *Père* attacks dueling and compares it to murder. This theme, popular in eighteenth century thought and literature, had already been dealt with by men such as Addison and Steele, Montesquieu, Rousseau, Voltaire, and Beccaria and would be taken up in Spain, not only in the famous play by Jovellanos, but also by Valladares in *Rufino y Aniceta* and *El vinatero de Madrid,* by Comella in *La Cecilia,* and in *El amante generoso* by Zavala y Zamora.

Even though the play consists of a series of «tableaux», it is less sentimental than other lachrymose comedies. Feeling, compassion and pity are exhibited but the moral discourses and sentimental verbiage, while not eliminated, are handled with discretion. Sedaine has a fine gift for natural dialogue.

I have examined a dramatic genre that was cultivated in England and

---

[31] MICHEL-JEAN SEDAINE, *Le Philosophe sans le savoir* (Paris: A. Hatier, 1929), 71.

on the continent, the main characteristics of which are a presentation of middle-class figures and an attempt not only to stir but to exploit the emotions of the audience and bring them to a point of view shared by the playwright. It is these characteristics and others discussed in this chapter that form the model against which we will study the contemporary lachrymose drama of Spain, and I have assembled a body of material that illustrates these characteristics.

CHAPTER III

THE HISTORIC AND CULTURAL BACKGROUND OF

THE *COMEDIA LACRIMOSA* IN SPAIN

The mood of sentimentalism, which had already gained control in England, France and Germany, also invaded Spanish thought and literature. Feijoo's essay, «Descubrimiento de una nueva facultad, ó potencia sensitiva en el hombre, á un philosofo,» was a proclamation of faith of this spirit of sensibility. This work was included in the fourth volume of his *Cartas eruditas y curiosas,* published in 1753. Since the third volume appeared in 1750, the essay was written sometime between 1750 and 1753. Spain was clearly part of the European mainstream of thought. Like Luzán and Padre Isla, Feijoo spoke of «el célebre Metaphysico inglés Juan Loke,», and his famous sensationalist epistemology.

This essay is Feijoo's declaration of belief in a sense other than the ones of sight, smell, touch, taste and hearing: «He discurrido ò pensado, que hay en nosotros una Potencia Sensitiva, ò llamese meramente Perceptiva, distinta de todas las demás...» (p. 78). To prove this point he makes the following argument: «Luego que oímos alguna noticia triste, ò vemos algun sucesso para nosotros lamentable, al punto se aflige el alma; y de la afliccion de el alma resulta promptamente en el cuerpo una especie de dolor congoxoso, que manifiestamente experimentamos en el pecho. La percepcion experimental de este dolor, ciertamente es una sensacion corporea. ¿Pero à qué sentido de los cinco pertenece? No parece possible adaptarle à alguno de ellos, sino por mera voluntariedad. Luego hay otro sentido corporeo innominado, à quien pertenece essa sensacion» (p. 86).

Not only does Feijoo write about this new spirit, but his very choice of words, seen for example in Letter VIII of the same volume, «Despotismo, ó dominio tiranico de la imaginacion,» reflects the sentimental, lachrymose and emotional tone then prevalent in European literature and painting: «lo que pasa en los que tienen el corazon mas sensible, ó el alma mas dispuesta, yá á los sentimientos de la ternura amatoria, yá de la compasion

---

[1] D. Fray Benito Gerónimo Feijoo y Montenegro, «Descubrimiento de una nueva facultad, ó potencia sensitiva en el hombre, á un philosofo,» in *Cartas eruditas y curiosas* (Madrid: Blas Román, 1781), Carta VI, IV, 79.

de los males agenos, yá a la estimacion afectuosa de las virtudes, ó aversion á los vicios que reconocen en otros, cuando leen una Comedia, una Novela, ó qualquiera Historia fabulosa; donde se representan con imagenes vivas, expresiones insinuantes, y descripciones patéticas, sucesos yá prosperos, yá adversos; empeños, ó pretensiones, yá de feliz, yá de infeliz éxito, yá virtudes amables, yá detestables vicios. Sin embargo de saber, y representarles el entendimiento, que toda aquella narracion es fabulosa, sin mezcla de un atomo de realidad, experimentan en su corazon todos aquellos afectos, que podrian producir los sucesos, siendo verdaderos y reales. Qué deseos de vér feliz á un Heroe de ilustres prendas! Qué sustos al contemplarle amenazado de algun revés de la fortuna! ¡Qué lastima ácia un objeto, y al mismo tiempo qué ira ácia otro, al representarseles maltratada una mujer virtuosa por un marido brutal! Qué complacencia, mezclada con admiracion, al exponerseles acciones proprias de una virtud excelsa! Qué enojos contra la fortuna, ó por mejor decir contra los siniestros dispensadores de ella, en la exaltacion de un malvado, y en el abatimiento de un sugeto de ilustre merito! » (pp. 112-113).

The sentimental view of man became so common that inevitably it appeared on the stage. The first mention of sentimental comedy in Spanish probably appeared in Ignacio de Luzán's brief sketch of Nivelle de la Chaussée in his *Memorias literarias de París* (1751). He approved of La Chaussée's excellent *comédies larmoyantes,* especially *Le Préjugé à la mode*: «M. de la Chaussée, de la Academia Francesa, es autor de excelentes comedias a quienes se les ha dado el epíteto de *larmoyantes* (llorosas) por los tiernos afectos que en ellas exprime con grande arte el autor. *Mélanide, La escuela de las madres (L'École des mères), La aya (La Gouvernante)* y el *Préjugé à la mode* son de este autor. Todas son muy buenas, y pueden competir con las más célebres que se hayan representado hasta ahora en parte alguna. Pero la última *(Le Préjugé à la mode)* está trabajada con un acierto, con un arte y con un gusto apenas imitable.»[2]

But as early as 1737, in the first edition of his *Poética,* Luzán spoke of the desirability of a type of dramatic production which profoundly moved the audience to sympathize with the joys and the sorrows of the *dramatis personae*: «Porque, sin embargo, que el auditorio sabe ya que aquel príncipe es fingido por pocas horas, que aquella desgracia es imitada, que aquel peligro es aparente, la buena imitación y, como dice Horacio, el mágico engaño de la poesía y de la dramática representación, hace de modo que los oyentes, llevados de un dulce hechizo, se apasionen por objetos fingidos como si fuesen verdaderos, y, preocupados en favor del primer papel por las prendas y virtudes con que le adorna el poeta, se interesen por él, se duelan de su aflicción, lloren en su desgracia, se asusten en su peligro y se alegren en su felicidad.»[3] Even though in the *Poética* he never names the genre *per se,* the emotional, sentimental bent of which he speaks, is the very foundation of sentimental comedy.

[2]   IGNACIO DE LUZÁN, *Memorias literarias de París* (Madrid, 1751), pp. 79-80.
[3]   IGNACIO DE LUZÁN, *La poética o reglas de la poesía en general y de sus principales especies,* ed. Luigi de Filippo (Barcelona: Selecciones Bibliófilas, 1956), II, 81.

Sentimental comedy was one of the main topics of conversation among literary men and scholars during Luzán's years in Paris, between 1747 and 1750. Luzán and many Spanish neo-classicists were willing to support this genre because it was didactic, it had a moral purpose, it obeyed the principle of verisimilitude with its simple arguments and faithful representation of people and themes from everyday life, and it could be composed within the guidelines of classic rules. Zavala y Zamora states, in the «Advertencia al lector» which was included in the 1797 edition of *Las víctimas del amor, Ana y Sindhám,* that this drama does not violate the basic neo-classic precepts: «la accion es una sola... El lugar de la Escena se extiende á Londres y sus cercanias, ensanche que dió, y aun ha seguido en muchas composiciones la religiosidad de nuestros preceptistas Franceses. Solo la unidad del tiempo padece alguna violencia por la precipitacion de la catástrofe.» They also approved of the fact that sentiment replaced ridicule.

Leandro Fernández de Moratín, speaking of *El delincuente honrado* in the *Discurso preliminar* to his plays, affirmed that «aunque demasiado distante del carácter de la buena comedia, se admiró en ella la expresión de los afectos, el buen lenguaje y la excelente prosa de su diálogo.»[4]

Jovellanos, in his *Memoria para el arreglo de la policía de los espectáculos y diversiones públicas y sobre su origen en España* (1790) approved of the basic tenets of lachrymose comedy. He emphasized the importance of plays which would instruct as well as entertain: «un espectáculo capaz de instruir ó extraviar el espíritu y de perfeccionar ó corromper el corazon de los ciudadanos.»[5] He wanted a theater of pedagogic intention in which sentiment and virtue were exalted: «un teatro... que iria tambien formando su corazon y cultivando su espiritu» (p. 496), a theater that «puede abrazar el espíritu y todos los sentimientos que pueden mover el corazon humano... un teatro que aleje los ánimos del conocimiento de la verdad, fomentando doctrinas y preocupaciones erróneas, ó que desvie los corazones de la práctica de la virtud, excitando pasiones y sentimientos viciosos, lejos de merecer la protección, merecerá el odio y la censura de la pública autoridad» (p. 495). Jovellanos also felt that these virtues should be demonstrated in middle-class citizens: «magistrados humanos é incorruptibles, ciudadanos llenos de virtud y de patriotismo, prudentes y celosos padres de familia, amigos fieles y constantes; en una palabra, hombres heróicos y esforzados, amantes del bien público, celosos de su libertad y sus derechos, y protectores de la inocencia y acérrimos perseguidores de la iniquidad» (p. 496).

Don Francisco María de Silva, pseudonym of Pedro Francisco de Luxán Silva y Góngora, Duque de Almodóvar, also spoke of the merits of this genre in his *Década epistolar sobre el estado de las letras en Francia* (1781): «son unos dramas que interesan, están llenos de sentimientos nobles, de

---

[4] LEANDRO FERNÁNDEZ DE MORATÍN, «Discurso preliminar a sus comedias,» in *Obras de Don Nicolás y de Don Leandro Fernández de Moratín,* B.A.E., II (Madrid, 1944), p. 319.

[5] D. GASPAR MELCHOR DE JOVELLANOS, «Memoria para el arreglo de la policía de los espectáculos y diversiones públicas y sobre su origen en España,» in *Obras,* B.A.E., XLVI (Madrid, 1951), p. 495.

pensamientos discretos bien ajustados; de una inquietud y un dulce patético que suspende y afecta el ánimo.»[6]

The genre had its beginnings in Spain in the celebrated *tertulia* of Olavide in Sevilla. Jovellanos and Cándido María Trigueros were two of the members. Jovellanos informs us, in the «Advertencia» to the 1787 edition of *El delincuente honrado,* that in the early part of 1773 there was a literary controversy in this tertulia over the *comédie larmoyante,* and as a result several members decided to have a contest, each one writing a *comedia lacrimosa.* Jovellanos won the prize for his play, *El delincuente honrado.*

John H. R. Polt affirms that *El delincuente honrado* «is the only one [of this group of *comedias lacrimosas*] to have survived.»[7] Jovellanos, in a letter of 1777 directed to the Abate de Valchrétien, was probably giving the reason why others were either lost or not made known: «Ni crea usted que el *Delincuente* es la única cosa que ha producido la imitacion de los buenos modelos. Yo conozco, y pudiera citar algunos dramas del mismo género escritos modernamente, que tienen un mérito muy sobresaliente; pero sus autores los guardan con mas cuidado que el que yo tuve con el mio, y se libran de muchas desazones, que á mi me ha costado su publicacion. Conocen que no ha llegado aun en el momento de entregar al público estos testimonios de sus útiles tareas, y se contentan con esperarle, fiando su desagravio a la posteridad.»[8] In this passage, Jovellanos definitely seems to be alluding to the other lachrymose comedies written as a result of this contest.[9]

In spite of Polt's affirmation and Jovellanos' reasoning, Russell P. Sebold has discovered another *comedia lacrimosa* undoubtedly written for the same contest, *El precipitado,* by Trigueros.[10] Francisco Aguilar Piñal, a scholar specializing in the life and work of Trigueros and the tertulia de Olavide,[11] affirms that Trigueros was a friend of Jovellanos and that «en sus frecuentes viajes a Sevilla participó en las tertulias de Olavide donde nació su dedicación al teatro.»[12]

---

[6] D. Francisco María de Silva, *Década epistolar sobre el estado de las letras en Francia,* 2nd ed. (1781; rpt. Madrid, 1792), p. 255.

[7] John H. R. Polt, *Gaspar Melchor de Jovellanos* (New York: Twayne Publishers, 1971), p. 68.

[8] D. Gaspar Melchor de Jovellanos, «Contestación a la carta dirigida al autor por el Abate de Valchrétien,» in *Obras,* B.A.E., XLVI, 81.

[9] Jean Sarrailh, in his article on *El delincuente honrado,* praised this work of Jovellanos and declared it superior to other *comedias lacrimosas* of the same epoch: «Il apparaît que le *Delincuente,* comparé à toutes les tentatives espagnoles du moment, demeure, dans son genre, la pièce qui présente le plus de mérites littéraires et qui, par le problème social qu'elle débat et l'émotion qu'elle crée, est sans doute la plus caractéristique et la plus honorable de la seconde moitié du XVIIIe siècle espagnol.» «A propos du *Delincuente honrado* de Jovellanos,» in *Mélanges d'Études Portugaises offerts à M. Georges Le Gentil* (Instituto para a alta cultura, 1949), p. 337.

[10] See his article, «El incesto, el suicidio y el primer romanticismo español,» *Hispanic Review,* 41, No. 4 (Autumn, 1973), 682.

[11] See his book, *La Sevilla de Olavide 1767-1778* (Sevilla, 1966).

[12] Francisco Aguilar Piñal, «La obra 'ilustrada' de don Cándido María Trigueros,» *Revista de literatura,* 34, Nos. 67-68 (July-December, 1968), 32.

The other principal dramatists of this genre in Spain were Luciano Francisco Comella, Antonio Valladares de Sotomayor, and Gaspar Zavala y Zamora. The great majority of the plays were written in the last three decades
of the eighteenth century, but as a genre it became even more popular in
the first half of the nineteenth century. Indeed, Antonio Gil y Zárate wrote a
comedia lacrimosa as late as 1843 entitled *Cecilia la cieguecita.*

Several of these sentimental comedies were imitations of *El delincuente
honrado.* Not only did they reproduce moral issues of honor, dignity and
dueling, but also specific details such as names of characters and specific
lines. For example, Don Anselmo is the devoted friend in *El bueno y el mal
amigo* and *El amor dichoso,* as well as *El delincuente honrado.* Valladares
copied the name of the enlightened judge, Don Justo de Lara, for his play *El
vinatero de Madrid.* As his namesake he is tolerant, prudent and generous. In
act V, scene vi of *El delincunente* Simon says: «Señores, cuanto pasa parece
una novela.» This same line is echoed by the sergeant at the end of *Rufino y
Aniceta*: «Esto es como una novela» and by Don Prudencio at the conclusion of *El precipitado*: «Me parece un sueño quanto pasa.» In all three
places the characters are underlining the extravagant, novelistic quality of
the action.

Most Spanish lachrymose comedies were imitations of English sentimental plays and novels, as well as French *comédies larmoyantes.* Don
Francisco María de Silva, in his *Década epistolar,* confirmed that the French
dramatists used the English sentimental novel as the source of arguments for
their plays: «la que merece mas particular atencion es la llamada *Comedie
Larmoyante…,* especie ò genero que puede llamarse nuevo, ò renovado con
mucha variedad y mayor correccion que antes, habiendo sacado la mayor
parte de asuntos o ideas de los romances ingleses.»[13] The fact that Spanish
dramatists did the same was confirmed in a review that appeared in the
Memorial literario in 1802: «Las innumerables novelas *sentimentales* con
que los ingleses y alemanes inundan la literatura europea dan nacimiento
a otros tantos dramas del mismo género, hechura y colorido, con que se
enriquecen los teatros; el nuestro ha recibido, y continúa recibiendo, un
refuerzo tan considerable de dramas modernos que, aunque a nosotros nos
cuesta casi tan poco trabajo en analizarlos y juzgarlos como a los autores
el componerlos, necesitaríamos sólo para dar razón de ellos la mayor parte
del tiempo que empleamos en la redacción de este periódico.»[14] Zavala y
Zamora, in the already cited «Advertencia al lector» of *Las víctimas del
amor, Ana y Sindhám,* declared that «el presente drama… es pensamiento
de una Novela Inglesa.» In Chapter II, I discussed the influence of many
English and French sentimental comedies on specific *comedias lacrimosas.*
It is interesting to note that Valladares and Závala y Zamora also wrote
sentimental novels in the English fashion, for example, *La Leandra,* of Va-

---

[13] pp. 251-252.
[14] 3rd. epoch, vol. II, p. 168. Quoted by Russell P. Sebold, in *El rapto de la
mente,* p. 51.

lladares (Madrid, 1797-1807), and *La Eumenia* of Zavala y Zamora (Madrid, 1805), as Russell P. Sebold has pointed out.[15]

Many *comedias lacrimosas* even take place in England and have characters with English names: *Eduardo y Federica,* «La escena en una quinta inmediata a una aldea de las cercanías de Londres,» with characters named Milord Donbay, Milord Derikson, Súmers, Derik; *Las víctimas del amor, Ana y Sindhám,* «La escena en Londres y sus cercanías,» with Milor Darambi, Sindhám, El Barón de Fronsvill; *El fabricante de paños o el comerciante inglés,* «La escena se representa en Londres,» with Wilson, Betzi, Milord Baltton, Milord Orcey; *El triunfo del amor y la amistad; Jenwal y Faustina,* «La acción pasa en Bristol,» with Darmont, Jenwal and Vangrey; *El casado avergonzado* by Comella, «La escena es en Londres,» with Sir Constante, Miladi Constante, Lovemore, Mrs. Lovemore, William Jonatam; *El amante honrado,* «La escena es en Londres,» with Sidney, Miladi Arnil, Beti, Falclán; and *El carbonero de Londres* which takes place in London («Edificios sumptuosos de la Corte de Londres y el Tamesis con alguna embarcacion anclada») with *dramatis personae* named Milord Rusban, Milord Gray, El Conde de Egremont, and Ricardo «en trage de trabajador inglés.»

The characteristics of this genre, as outlined by Diderot and practiced by English and French sentimental dramatists, found sanction in the main in the *comedia lacrimosa* in Spain.

The belief that the natural emotions of ordinary middle-class critizens are virtuous and deserve to be portrayed sympathetically is a prime tenet of sentimentalism. These *comedias lacrimosas* find their subjects in bourgeois life and conventions. They treat themes which reflect some somber aspect of everyday life and the problems are dealt with in the confines of familial, professional, and comercial relationships. While Romantic drama will attempt to transcend the mundane to find the ideal; the *comedia urbana* centers its attention on the mundane.

Another outstanding characteristic of this genre is its didactic, moralizing character. The desire to reform, to set the human heart in harmony with principles of virtue produced moral plays. Jovellanos, Trigueros, Valladares, Comella and Zavala y Zamora felt the theater was an excellent instrument for the propagation of the highest forms of conduct and morality. In most cases their theses are well integrated into the play; there is a logical development of the lesson in the plot. However, the didactic goal usually does irreparable harm to the characterization of the *dramatis personae.* Generally, the characters are one-dimensional, either excessively good or exceedingly evil. In most cases the moral is clearly stated at the end in the form of a maxim. With its intention to teach, sentimental comedy is a precursor of the nineteenth century social and thesis drama of playwrights like Scribe, Augier and Dumas *fils* in France, Tamayo y Baus and Adelardo López de Ayala in Spain.[16]

---

[15] *El rapto de la mente,* p. 50.

[16] It is interesting to note that J. Hunter Peak, in his book *Social Drama in Nineteenth-Century Spain* (Chapel Hill: University of North Carolina Press, 1964), declares that «the seed of social drama did not find fertile ground in the eighteenth

These dramas, with their emphasis on the individual and their sentiments, attack established society. The criticism of existing social conditions is found in three main areas in Spain: an attack on the corruption of the nobility and their pride; an attack on various laws and edicts; and an attack on customs such as arranging marriages that violated the wishes of the partners. Because of concern with the latter social convention, a common theme of these plays is the revolt of children against rigid, oppressive parents. The *comedia lacrimosa* champions a new moral code founded on friendship, tolerance, humanity and charity.

With this new concept of morality comes a new notion of the hero. He possesses qualities which are both virtuous (if viewed from the standpoint of the individual, the enemy of tradition) and sinful (if viewed according to the values and mores of conservative society). The virtuous man is the «noble savage.» Society is responsible for man's sins and transgressions.

These plays instruct through an appeal to the heart. The characters have a heightened and highly emotional response to events, actions and sentiments. The emotional stress of these middle-class people is intended to arouse the spectator's pity and suspense in advance of the approaching happy ending. Pantomime, optically impressive «tableaux,» emotionally charged monologues and an exclamatory, sentimental style add to the moving, often maudlin tone. In this respect in particular, these plays are also precursory to Romantic drama, and the «noble savage» will, of course, reappear in the Romantic theater, too.

The fusion of these characteristics makes it evident that we are dealing with a new genre of tragi-comedy.

century» (p. 141). It is hard to imagine plays more ethical in purpose, more social and moral in orientation than the *comedias lacrimosas*. It is their *raison d'être*.

Chapter IV

JOVELLANOS AND *EL DELINCUENTE HONRADO*

El delincuente honrado (1773) was one of the first lachrymose comedies written in Spain and is, undoubtedly, one of the best examples of the genre. The play exemplifies the change of literary techniques and moral tendencies that were prevalent in Spain in the final decades of the eighteenth century. As was noted in Chapter III, Jovellanos wanted a didactic theater in which sentiments and virtues might predominate. He was writing for a public intensely interested in political, judicial and social questions. In its concern for the bourgeoisie and their sentiments, with virtues demonstrated in middle-class citizens, *El delincuente honrado* calls into question existing social and judicial conventions. The play is clearly the product of an age of sensibility, sympathy, sentimentality, humanitarianism and fraternalism. This new morality is beautifully exemplified in Anselmo, Torcuato's dear friend who is willing to sacrifice his life for Torcuato. Because sentimental dramatists believed in the goodness of human nature, they believed they could change the moral outlook and open the way for moral reform. Above all, they insisted on happiness.

Jovellanos was greatly influenced by Beccaria in his advocation of humanitarian treatment for the criminal, in his censure of torture and in his condemnation of the anti-dueling laws. He was also affected by Beccaria's impassioned, sentimental style. Jovellanos will use sentiment and emotion as a constant tool of suasion. Laura appeals to her father's feelings:

> Padre mio, estoy muy segura de su inocencia; no, Torcuato no es merecedor de los viles títulos con que afeais su conducta... vos sois mi padre, y no podeis abandonarme. Pero si vuestro corazon resiste á mis suspiros, yo iré á lanzarlos á los piés del señor don Justo; su alma piadosa se enternecerá con mis lagrimas; le ofreceré mi vida por redimir la de mi esposo; y si no pudiese salvarle, morirémos juntos, pues yo no he de sobrevivir á su desgracia
>
> (act III, scene vi).

SIMÓN:

> *(Enternecido.)* ¡Pobrecita!... Sosiégate, hija mia, y no te abandones al dolor con tanto extremo.
> *(Aparte.)* Sus lágrimas me enternecen... (act III, scene vii).

49

When Don Justo receives the royal decree regarding Torcuato's fate, he declares: «Iré á bañar los piés del mejor de los reyes con mis humildes lágrimas» (act IV, scene vii).

El delincuente honrado demonstrates the basic tenet of sentimentalism; namely, the innate goodness of humanity. Because man is fundamentally good he can be moved: «Si las lágrimas son efecto de la sensibilidad del corazon, ¡desdichado de aquel que no es capaz de derramarlas!» (act I, scene iii). All the characters feel pity for the sufferings of Torcuato, and his virtue is rewarded in the end. Don Justo describes his own anguish when confronted with Torcuato's destiny: «Las lágrimas me ahogan...» (act V, scene i). He continues to express his sympathetic feelings: «¡Ah!, nosotros, infelices, que quedamos sumidos en un abismo de afliccion y miseria.» Anselmo describes the King's compassion when he, Anselmo, went to plead for Tocuato's life: «¡Ah, qué monarca tan piadoso! ¡Yo vi correr tiernas lágrimas de sus augustos ojos!» (act V, scene vii).

But *El delincuente honrado* deals with more than a narrow social issue. Rather, it treats a very broad philosophic one that is not only relevant to modern societies but is, indeed, one of their central concerns. For the play is not merely a polemic about the laws against dueling, as Jovellanos declared,[1] but the nature of laws and how men relate to them—both those who are being subjected to them, and, on a more sophisticated level, those who are charged with their administration. The playwright's bias is easy to identify. From a humanistic and enlightened position, he attacks those elements of law that are inflexible and unable to make distinctions among objective behavior based on the motive and character of the actor. He is equally contemptuous of judges who place fidelity to the cold words of a statute above the claims of compassion and understanding for those who are subject to such statutes.

This polemic is played out by two judges, Don Justo de Lara and Don Simón de Escobedo, and so contemporary is the issue that one could borrow the demagogic, political jargon of our time and call Don Simón, the strict constructionist and Don Justo, the judicial activist.

Don Simón is an intolerant and prejudiced man: «¡Gitanos!... ¡Fuego!» (act II, scene ii); endowed with a limited talent: «Estos discursos» he says to Don Justo, «son demasiado profundos; yo no soy filósofo ni los entiendo» (act IV, scene vi); harsh and conservative in his approach to the law: «Yo quisiera á los ministros mas duros, mas enteros... Hijo mio, ¡si tú hubieras alcanzado á los ministros de mi tiempo!... ¡Oh!, aquellos sí que eran hombres en forma! ¡Qué teoricones! Cada uno era un *Digesto* vivo. ¿Y su entereza? Vaya, no se puede ponderar. Entonces se ahorcaban hombres á docenas» (act I, scene v); who does not believe that it is the province of the judge to ameliorate the short-comings of the lawgiver, but only to serve the legislator.

---

[1] «Siendo el objeto de este drama descubrir la dureza de las leyes, que, sin distincion de provocado y provocante, castigan á los *duelistas* con pena capital.» «Contestación a la carta dirigida al autor por el Abate de Valchrétien,» in *Obras*, B.A.E., XLVI, 79.

Don Justo carries out the will of the legislator, because that is his obligation, but he also recognizes the defects of barbarous laws and edicts and the need to reform them. He speaks of «el rigor de las leyes» (act III, scene viii) and laments their inflexibility and oppressiveness in regard to the innocent:[2]

> Pero las leyes están decisivas. ¡Oh leyes! ¡Oh, duras é inflexibles leyes! En vano gritan la razon y la humanidad en favor del inocente... Y ¿seré yo tan cruel, que no exponga al Soberano?... No; yo le representaré en favor de un hombre honrado, cuyo delito consiste solo en haberlo sido (act III, scene x).

While giving his concept of honor, he, too, criticizes the laws on dueling as they then existed in Spain and the need to distinguish between the provoked and the provoker:[3]

> Bien sé que el verdadero honor es el que resulta del ejercicio de la virtud y del cumplimiento de los propios deberes. El hombre justo debe sacrificar á su conservacion todas las preocupaciones vulgares... Para un pueblo de filósofos seria buena la legislacion que castigase con dureza al que admite un desafío, que entre ellos fuera un delito grande. Pero en un país donde la educacion, el clima, las costumbres, el genio nacional y la misma constitucion inspiran á la nobleza estos sentimientos fogosos y delicados á que se da el nombre de pundonor; en un país donde el mas honrado es el menos sufrido, y el mas valiente el que tiene mas osadía; en un país, en fin, donde á la cordura se llama cobardía, y á la moderacion falta de espíritu, ¿será justa la ley que priva de la vida á un desdichado solo porque piensa como sus iguales; una ley que solo podrán cumplir los muy virtuosos ó los muy cobardes? (act IV, scene vi).

All our sympathies are enlisted on the side of Don Justo because his responses are humane («La virtud y generosidad de don Torcuato excitan mi compasion» (act III, scene viii). But while the issue treated in this play is both broad and compelling, the treatment is superficial.

As a polemic it weakens the drama and as a drama, it weakens the polemic. The dramatic force of the play drives us toward the identification of a problem —the unjust nature of inflexible laws— but the polemical thrust suggests remedies and such suggestions are beyond the province of the dramatic form. For, to have jurists stand for the conflicting points of view on this issue, one would have to turn away from human aspirations and demands, which are the concern of drama, to questions of remedy and procedure which are the stuff of tightly reasoned legal briefs.

In spite of sharing all the dramatic shortcomings of the genre and its narrow treatment of the theme it presents, the play, nevertheless, stands out because of what it attempts, and, read with attention and care, speaks in part to the modern reader.

[2] Torcuato, while condemning the use of torture to extract a confession, also voices his extreme dissatisfaction with existing judicial conditions: «¿Es posible que en un siglo en que se respeta la humanidad y en que la filosofía derrama su luz por todas partes, se escuchen aún entre nosotros los gritos de la inocencia oprimida?» (act V, scene v).
[3] Since the beginning of the eighteenth century, Spanish kings had passed severe laws against dueling. As recently as April 28, 1757, Fernando VI had published an edict.

CHAPTER V

THE REJECTION OF DIDACTICISM IN
CÁNDIDO MARÍA TRIGUEROS' *EL PRECIPITADO*

El precipitado (1773),[1] with its declamatory speeches, direct appeal to emotion and moral orientation, is not only very much in the tradition of the lachrymose comedy, but also an important antecedent of Spanish Romantic drama. It is a transitory work which lays the groundwork for themes and styles found in the theater sixty years later.

The play can be considered an attack on established society. The anguish of the protagonist, Don Amato, is not the result of adverse occurrences or wicked characters, but rather of laws and social injustices which oppress him.

All the characters are sensitive, virtuous beings and the pursuit of happiness is a constant goal with each of them. Doña Gracia, Amato's aunt, speaks of Cándida's «afable ternura» and her feelings «que sale[n] del corazon» (act I, scene i). Don Prudencio, Amato's father, cannot resist Cándida's «virtud.» Don Amato assures Cándida, his beloved, that her lack of money will not prevent his family from loving her: «No te canses, Cándida: todos los mios te conocen: aprecian la virtud mas que el oro: y yo a ti sobre todo» (act II, scene i).

Don Amato is described by Cándida as

> el egemplar de los Jóvenes nobles;... El Señor Don Amato es el mancebo mas bien hecho, mas bien educado, mas generoso que tiene Sevilla: el Señor Don Amato es el mas cortes, el mas atento::: ¡Que corazon el del Señor Don Amato, que corazon tan de acuerdo con sus palabras! Solo le sirven los labios del corazón. El Señor Don Amato ... es la persona mas digna del pueblo   (act I, scene i).

Don Prudencio is also a decent, praiseworthy man. His attitudes towards marrying Cándida, whom he loves with great passion, reflect the tolerance and humanity exalted in the Age of Enlightenment:

> Io no estoi seguro del amor de Cándida; aunque lo estè de su resignacion: si la pobre casase conmigo sin amarme, io que solo deseo su bien, no lograría

[1] This play was entitled *Cándida o la hija sobrina*, in the 1774 manuscript (Madrid: Biblioteca Nacional) and *El precipitado*, in the edition of 1785 (London: British Museum).

52

otra cosa que hacer mas pesada su infelicidad... Io serè dichoso si me ama: : : serè infeliz si no soi amado; pero a lo menos no tendrè la desdicha de contribuir a la suia... La prudencia es el alma de la vida humana: i mucho mas necesaria en cosas tan importantes (act II, scene iv).

Cándida appreciates Prudencio's righteous character: «generosidad sin ejemplo!» (act III, scene vii). Prudencio, in turn, assures Cándida that she will always find in him «el ternísimo corazon de un padre» (act III, scene viii).

The characters are guided by their hearts and natural instincts to truth, right conduct and happiness. From these liberated emotions emerges a new type of being, not rational, but sensitive, compassionate, tender, humane and generous. The playwrights are interested in portraying the flow and fluctuations of feelings, sentiments and passions of these «sensitive souls.» This is one of the most highly charged *comedias lacrimosas*. To be virtuous one must be sympathetic, and all the characters exhibit great sentiment, emotion and sensitivity. Tears flow freely.[2] The play consists of a series of moving soliloquies, «tableaux vivants,» and touching scenes of recognition with all the gesturing and posturing recommended by Diderot as essential to work on the sentiments of the audience. The use of pantomime also enhances the sentimental force of the play.[3] The scene in which Don Amato goes before his father to ask permission to marry Cándida is an excellent example of trying to effect man's conduct by appealing to his emotions:

Me ha presentado [speaking of Candida] mil inconvenientes, i no se dexa vencer de mis razones ... Me ha ponderado vuestros favores, me ha dicho que la teneis casada. Vuestros beneficios, dice, la tienen cautiva: no puede ser sino de quien vos la mandeis: : puede dexar de ser mia ... puede ser infeliz; pero no puede ser
   Don Prudencio mui enternecido vuelve a un lado el rostro, i se cubre con la mano.
ingrata: : : aih, Señor, bolveis a otra parte el rostro? huis de vuestro desolado hijo?: : : A vuestros pies
   (Se arroja a los pies del padre)
espirarè, si despues de mis infortunios encuentro crueldad en el corazon de mi padre. Sino os parece que es digna mi eleccion: : : mas ¿como podreis negar que es la mas acertada?: : Si quereis castigar mi furor, mi precipitacion, mi desobediencia, abandonadme, castigadme, desheredadme: dad mis bienes a esa prima desconocida, i hacedla feliz: conservadme solamente a Cándida, i vuestro amor ... dadme vuestra aprobacion, dadme vuestra bendicion para que sea suio:
   (El Padre se enternece mas, llora, i lo vè el hijo)
nada mas os pido: esta mi sola súplica: : : Ah!
   (con vehemencia)
vencimos Cándida, vencimos, llora mi caro Padre (act II, scene v).

---

[2] Consider these words of Cándida as an example: «Lloro, Señor, lloro la desgracia de mi suerte, que me hace infeliz con la misma felicidad» (act II, scene i).
[3] The following is one of many examples: *«Don Amato sale precipitadamente, i se arroja llorando a los pies de su padre; el padre le levanta enternecido, i le abraza»* (act III, scene viii).

The dynamics of this play distinguish it from the genre. For where we have shown the use to which sentiment and emotion were put by the plays of the genre, we have a drama whose *raison d'être* is emotionalism. It is not a question of showing how unjust laws oppress virtuous individuals, but of how a law with the broadest consensual support, the law against incest, can cause unhappiness to individuals who mistakenly believe they have violated it. The playwright certainly had no aspirations to move his audience emotionally so as to bring them to a point of view opposing laws against incest, a position that would not have been credible or acceptable at that time in Spain. His only aim was to have his audience cry. By opposing a law seen as just, and therefore good, against individuals who are praiseworthy, the play seems to be putting elements with equal claims on our sympathy in opposition. This structure could be the basis for a tragedy in the Aristotelian sense. But any such force is dissipated because the protagonists are not really incestuous at all, as I shall show now. Compare the impact of the following feeble dénouement with that of Oedipus who really was incestuous!

The theme of incest is introduced when Doña Marcela, the long-absent mother of Amato, returns to Sevilla and announces that Cándida is her daughter and therefore the sister of Amato.[4] Don Amato, already married to Cándida, is horrified at the news: «Su hija!:: mi hermana!:: que horror!» (act IV, scene iv). Amato laments being the victim of a society whose inflexible laws will not permit him the liberty of loving whom he chooses:

> Perdiera io primero la vida, que ser de otra, sino puedo ser de Cándida ... Las leies, fuertes leies! las leies me roban el ùnico bien que apetecía::: ... lo privado sin remedio de la que adoro! Io esposo de mi hermana! Io ...
>
> (act IV, scene v).

Longing for the voluptuousness of the Orient, where there are less restrictions on man's natural instincts, Amato exclaims

> ¡porque no naci io en los paises del Oriente, donde no es delito amar a sus hermanas los tiernos hermanos? Io no la puedo poseer!:: Io no la puedo dexar de amar: no puedo:: no hai remedio:::
>
> *(Se dexa caer sobre un sillon)*
>
> Muramos, pues:: mi delito, i mi desventura estan en no olvidarla:: pongamos fin a mi delito:: ... i mi alma?: ah!: mi alma?::: eternamente infeliz.
>
> *(Levantase con furor)*
>
> Cara madre, despues de quince años de esclavitud, havras logrado la libertad para venir a morir de dolor rebolcada en la sangre de tu hijo! ... de tu hijo criminal! de tu hijo incestuoso! ... Incestuoso! terrible idea! o virtud! o delito!
>
> (act V, scene i).

---

[4] The play is full of mystery and suspense with lost-personages and confused identities due to a series of captivities, shipwrecks and other episodes endured in the Orient.

Prudencio, too, is horrified at his incestuous love: «Si hijo, tù::: Mi dolor no es menor que el vuestro: mi amada hija, mi hija cuio esposo quise ser:: me horrorizo al recordarlo::: (act IV, scene vi).

While this work does not oppose or even seriously bring into question the laws against incest, the sympathy it attempts to elicit from its audience through the use of emotionalism sets in progress attitudes that put the burden of proof on society whenever it adopts laws, customs, and conventions that stand between the populace and their impulses.

CHAPTER VI

THE SENTIMENTAL COMEDIES OF
ANTONIO VALLADARES DE SOTOMAYOR

Valladares' *comedias lacrimosas* often present the world of finance, commerce and trade, and are therefore antecedents of the «alta comedia» of the nineteenth century. Within this framework issues of conscience, such as honor, fortune and dignity, are discussed. The attack on established society, by showing the interplay between the nobility and the middle-class and the right to choose one's mate in marriage are the two most prevalent themes in his lachrymose comedies.

El fabricante de paños o el comerciante inglés (1783) [1] presents the domestic misfortunes of Wilson, a cloth-merchant. Act I takes place in his office in London: «El teatro representa el despacho de Wilson, con varios taburetes repartidos con orden por los lados: en el derecho del foro habrá una puerta que se supone vá al almacen; otra en medio que dirige á la tienda... habrá un bufete con varios papeles y escribania.» Immediately we are struck by the realistic touches of the stage-set. These sets, typical of all *comedias lacrimosas*, serve as models for the vivid scenes of local color which will characterize Spanish Romantic drama. Indeed, they are typical of eighteenth century Spanish literature in general with its emphasis on the picturesque and its interest in accurate, concrete description.

This play is a perfect example of the genre. We are looking at a work that is essentially a polemic on a narrow social issue: the bankruptcy laws as they were then administered in Spain. The author's goal, to cause his audience to feel these laws to be harsh and unjust,[2] and the means he employs, the unceasing manipulations of their emotions and sympathies,[3]

---

[1] This play was based on Lillo's *The London Merchant*.

[2] Wilson has just lost 3000 pounds sterling because the House of Sudmer, in which his money was deposited, has gone bankrupt. Six bailiffs arrive and demand immediate payment for his creditors. Since Wilson cannot pay, they remove all his belongings from his office, shop and store.

[3] Consider this touching *tableau*: «Los seis oficiales de Vilson, [upon seeing the bailiffs remove his possessions] salen por la puerta del almacen con delantales, y cruzan la scena para ir á la tienda, caminando lentamente, los brazos caidos, las cabezas vajas, y en una profunda tristeza» (act II). All the characters cry over Wilson's misfortune. One of the officials of Wilson's factory says: «Oh, mi querido Señor! / Nosotros solo lloramos / por vos. Vuestra situacion / produce nuestro que-

are completely subordinate to any interest in writing a coherent play. We sympathize with Wilson only because of his distress. He is, in fact, a very small man caught up in his own self-pity [4] in spite of the fact that his financial reverses brought with them a demonstration of love, devotion, tolerance and charity from his family, friends and employees that would have been ample support for any character with whom an audience could really become engaged.

Fania, Wilson's second wife, gives Villianz, the one wicked character in the play, her valuable earrings as payment for her husband's debt, without Wilson's knowing it. Wilson's daughter willingly and lovingly gives up her diamond necklace in an effort to help her father reclaim some of his possessions:

> Papá mio, mi collar,
> la sangre que circulando
> está en mis venas, mi tierno
> corazon, mi vida, quanto
> tengo, y puedo tener,
> es todo vuestro   (act II).

Wilson's employees have also rounded up the small jewels they own and sold them, giving the proceeds to Wilson as a sign of love and loyalty. Finally Fania tries to comfort her husband, insisting that although they are without material wealth, they still possess love and virtue, the important qualities of life.

The final act takes place in the square in front of Westminster Bridge. Wilson vacillates between looking for the home of a man who is willing to give him a substantial sum of money as a gift and taking his life in the moonlit Thames. He meets a man to whom he tells his story of desperation. This man informs him that he would gladly trade his wealthy status for Wilson's poor one and scolds Wilson for his defeatist attitude:

> Hombre bárbaro, el que piensa
> como tú! Que estas creyendo
> que la desesperacion
> es valor? Pues no: es efecto
> de una alma debil: baxeza
> del ánimo, y verdadero
> caracter del que es cobarde:
> ... Tú tienes
> muger virtuosa, hijos vellos,
> y porque Dios te ha quitado
> lo que te dió, quitas á ellos
> un padre, un esposo, un dulce
> asilo en su desconsuelo   (act IV).

branto» (act II). In the same act Wilson, with tears in his eyes, begs the bailiffs to at least leave behind the money they have found in a box so that he can pay his faithful employees their week's salary. They refuse.

[4] Wilson, feeling ashamed and completely distraught plans to commit suicide. The set accentuates his somber, gloomy mood: «El teatro estará obscuro por ser la scena de noche. Sale Wilson por la izquierda trayendo una luz, que pondrá sobre la mesa, caminando con la mas profunda tristeza» (act III).

In a moving scene of recognition, Wilson then learns that this is Milord Baltton of Scotland, father of Fania and the lover who abandonned Fania's mother. Baltton, thrilled to know that Madama Sambrig and his daughter are alive and well and feeling remorse for his past actions, pays off Wilson's creditors and announces his plan to marry Sambrig, who now feels her honor has been restored.

Not only are the virtuous rewarded, but also the wicked are punished. Villianz, the hypocritical friend who demanded payment from Wilson at a time he could least afford it, is turned over to the local authorities for imprisonment when Baltton informs the judge of the crimes Villianz committed in Scotland. «Ya veo / que este es un justo castigo / de mis infamias;» says Villianz. Baltton adds:

> ... que asi
> sabe dar el justo Cielo
> á las maldades castigo,
> y á las virtudes el premio   (act IV)

a principle faithfully observed in this genre.

The characters in this play are the merest of pawns to its purpose. The play, of course, is a dismal dramatic failure [5] and survives only as a curiosity. This is inevitable, not necessarily because of the playwright's lack of skill, but because of his purpose which was didactic and political rather than artistic.

El trapero de Madrid combines the problems of the world of commerce with the theme of choosing one's mate. The treatment of marriage as an affair of love rather than of marriage settlements is typically sentimental. The dramatist attempts to present the thesis, frequently expounded in these lachrymose comedies, that true nobility rests in deeds (el tío Agustín) and not titles (Don Anselmo).

Don Basilio is a successful businessman in the wool industry. In spite of the fact that Don Anselmo is a man repulsive to his daughter, Don Basilio insists on marrying this old, but rich nobleman to her in order to elevate his own social station. Bernardo, Basilio's secretary and sweetheart of Rita, Basilio's daughter, laments his master's false values when he rejects him as a son-in-law because he is the son of poor, but virtuous rag dealer, el tío Agustín:

> su buen Padre, y mi Señor
> es poderoso en extremo,
> y de gran fama en la Corte.
> Y qué es el mio? un Trapero
> infeliz! un hombre honrado;
> pero que tiene un grosero

---

[5] In spite of my negative assessment, given the great popularity of sentimentalism in the eighteenth century, these *Comedias lacrimosas* were often box office successes. Santos Díez González affirmed that «luego que salieron al teatro las que se llaman 'tragedias urbanas' fueron por lo común bien recibidas y aplaudidas.» (*Instituciones poéticas,* IV, Madrid: Cano, 1793, p. III).

exercicio; y qué no es digna
la virtud de todo aprecio?
Es verdad. Pues en mi Padre
siempre está reinando: luego
por qué el mundo desestima
tan grande merecimiento?   (act I).

Anselmo is a calculating, conniving man whose «love» for Rita is commensurate with the size of her dowry: «Mi afecto / llegará á un millon de grados, / si lleba un millon de pesos» (act I). Basilio is a pretentious fool who, in spite of the fact he had many previous warnings, only recognizes Anselmo's perverse, cruel and avaricious nature when Anselmo refuses to lend him money at a time of financial reverses. It is at that time that the disillusioned Basilio tells Agustín: «ahora comprendo: que la amistad de este mundo, / es solamente el dinero» (act II). Agustín, the prudent, upright man who is content with his lot in life, shares his wisdom with Basilio: «que la nobleza mejor / es la virtud» (act II).

The play is absurd. Nothing really happens. Is virtue rewarded? Does Basilio really learn a lesson? It turns out that Agustín is a very wealthy man in spite of his modest trade, and when the creditors arrive to attach Basilio's goods, he gladly pays off Basilio's large debt. Basilio finally agrees to marry Rita to Bernardo. Rather than the thesis being that virtue lies in good deeds, you could say that money lies in odd places. Basilio still gets his way in the end because he marries his daughter to money. These plays are extremely provincial.

The same comments hold true for *Rufino y Aniceta*.[6] While basically sentimental in the sense that the heroes who are given virtuous characteristics get what they want in the end, these works in no sense undercut the prejudices they attack. They are especially dismal failures in this regard because in fact they support these prejudices. Rufino, a poor apprentice of Cosme, does not get to marry Aniceta, Cosme's daughter, until he is rich. The prejudiced parents get exactly what they wanted. The nature of the reward in these plays is wealth.

The dramatist also seems to be criticizing the conspiracy laws as they existed in Spain at that time. The prejudices of society which favor wealth and station, and which are supposedly under attack in this play, transform the character of the hero from one that was prudent, generous and loving to one that is bitter and vindictive. Rufino decides to challenge Casimiro, his rival for the hand of Aniceta, to a duel and states his intentions in a letter. He muses about «la satisfaccion sangrienta / y criminal que he resuelto» (act II). The unmailed letter of challenge to Casimiro, which had been discovered by the authorities, is the basis of Rufino's arrest. Even though Rufino declares that he had later realized how horrendous his intention was and had written another letter retracting his challenge, it is only through the benevolence of Casimiro that he is freed.

---

[6] The author of this play is listed as D. Anastasio Valderosal y Montedoro. This pseudonym is a near anagram for Antonio Valladares de Sotomayor.

The arrest for the writing of an unmailed letter suggests a notion of conspiracy laws in Spain that went far beyond the concept of such laws known to Anglo-American law. An enlightened criminal code distinguishes between a man's conduct and his intention, the concept being that while a man's conduct may be the concern of the state, his thoughts, and therefore the integrity of his personality, should be beyond its reach.

El vinatero de Madrid (1784) is a very poor play. The characters are one-dimensional, and none of the action is faithful to any psychological motivation. The drama is completely manipulative to make people cry, but it even fails within its own goals. While attempting to criticize the institution of dueling, the character who is treated most sympathetically turns out to be an arch-duelist.

It is one of several *comedias lacrimosas* which glorify middle-class life by presenting the interaction between this class and the nobility. While criticizing many social conventions of the times, it attempts to exalt virtue, friendship, tolerance and charity as the true tenets of dignity and happiness.

The drama takes place in the impoverished home of Juan, a poor, but virtuous wine-merchant and presents a stage-set filled with realistic details: «salon largo pobre, cuyo fondo ocuparan algunas sillas viejas, una arca inferior, una masa pequeña: sobre ésta habrá una capa parda, y montera, y á un lado una espada antigua: en cada extremo del foro habrá varios pellejos, unos vacíos, y otros que se suponen llenos de vino...; un embudo grande sobre una silla, y sobre otra un esportillo y un canastillo con ropa aplanchada, una cuerda cruzará el Teatro cerca del telon, y en ella se verá ropa blanca colgada para secarse.»

As the play opens an unhappy Juan sees in hard work both virtue and honor:

> Hija, mas pesan mis culpas,
> y siempre acuestas las llevo.
> Mira, quando cuesta el pan
> mas sudor, luego al comerlo
> es mas delicado, mas
> dulce, y hace mas provecho.
> Cada uno tiene su cruz.
> ... ...
> Llevemos con gusto nuestra
> cruz, y no solo la harémos
> agradable, sino que
> después Dios nos dará el premio   (act I).

Implied in his words, of course, is a condemnation of aristocratic improductivity, Juan feels his honor at stake when he learns that the Marqués del Prado has seduced his daughter Angelita and has gone back on his word to marry her. « ¡Mi honor ha muerto! » This notion of lost honor sets the the moral tone of the play. We, the audience, immediately feel pity for Juan's sufferings because of his fine character. Angelita pleads with the

Marquis, kneeling with tears in her eyes,[7] to change his decision. He refuses
to marry her, in spite of the fact that he gave her a legal document stating his
intention. He justifies his breaking his promise on the grounds that they
are of different social stations and that his uncles have chosen another
partner for him. In essence, the Marquis is a decent man who really does
love Angelita but is led astray by social prejudices and his wicked friend
Nicasio:

> Es cierto,
> Don Nicasio: mas mi amor: : :
> su virtud: : : mis juramentos: : :
> aquella inocencia: : aquella
> hermosura: : :
> ... Pero el Mundo: : :   (act I).

As one can see from this speech, the exclamatory, sentimental style, characteristic of the genre, is beautifully exemplified in this particular play.
Juan's predicament gives rise to social commentaries on the worth of the
nobility:

> De qué sirve la nobleza
> sin buenos procedimientos?
> Si á la virtud no conoce,
> y la persigue, es lo mesmo
> que un sol eclipsado, pues
> pierde así su lucimiento   (act I).

Juan decides that he, too, will appeal to the Marquis to carry out his
promise: «...mi llanto, / regando las plantas vuestras, / de vos lo aguarda,
Señor» (act I). When the Marquis again states the impossibility, despite his
love for her («pero mis tios: : mi amigo: : / mi honor: : ») Juan challenges
him to a duel. The Marquis does not wish to accept the challenge from an old
man but Juan insists. Juan succeeds in unarming the Marquis but does not
kill him. Hoping that the Marquis will marry his daughter, he suspends
the duel. Finally, with sword in hand, Juan takes his case before the newly
arrived local judge, Don Justo de Lara. Justo is very moved by Juan's
situation: «Mis lágrimas no las puedo / contener» (act II). It is true that
all of these plays place a high moral value on sympathy and benevolence,
but what is the reason behind this extreme empathy? An element of suspense and mystery is added to the plot. After Justo orders the Marquis to
fulfill his promise, «ser noble, / y proceder mal, yo creo / que es mala
nobleza,» Juan reveals that he, too, is a nobleman and a Caballero de
Santiago. As Juan continues to relate his life story Justo recognizes Juan

---

[7] «Pues con ternezas, suspiros, / y lágrimas os lo ruego. / ... Ah, Marqués mío!
Mirad / mi afliccion, y desconsuelo. / Enjugad mi triste llanto, / vuestras promesas
cumpliendo» (act I).

to be his father that he has not seen for so many years.[8] Juan has been traveling in a state of disguise because many years earlier, while defending his honor, he killed a man. Justo now has the difficult task of having to imprison his own father.

The play does have a happy dénouement. Juan is freed when a letter is discovered granting him pardon for his crime; Angelita will marry the Marquis and Nicasio is imprisoned for his crimes. Once again the principle of «poetic justice» is demonstrated. «Quien ofende á la virtud,» says Nicasio «siempre será castigado» (act II).

Concerning the theme of recognition, this play contains two elements referred to earlier in this study. First we have a discovery of identity concerning a father and son which is not only a common dramatic device in this genre but part of a very basic myth concerning the uncertainty of parentage that reflects itself in religious beliefs as well as in literature. The second element of discovery concerns the revelation that the bourgeois Juan is a noble. By including this latter example I am using the concept of recognition to cover all elements in these plays, wherein the true identity or station of a character turns out to be other than what was first anticipated, and the discovery is made by the audience and characters simultaneously.

The interesting thing about this technique is not only that it tends to stir emotion but that it is particularly suited to a genre aimed at the bourgeois or newly liberated class. Discovering wealth, nobility or children, where it appeared there was none, stressed the varied possibilities of existence and by inference the logic and need for mobility and flexibility in society.

La Adelina (1781), one of the less tearful sentimental comedies, is another play that shows the interation of the nobility and the middle-class. The bourgeois characters are virtuous, and the aristocratic ones are divided among the wicked (Baron de Tezél) and the honorable and enlightened (Emperador).[9] The play is about honor.

---

[8] This is a typical scene of recognition frequently found in these plays.

> JUSTO. Me llamo
> Don Justo de Lara y Silba.
>
> JUAN. Qué he' escuchado!
> Hijo de mi corazon!
> *(Se arroja á sus brazos.)*
> ... Querido Justo,
> á tu Padre estás mirando.
>
> JUSTO. Ah Padre mio! En el seno
> de mi corazon entraos.
> (act II).

[9] «Un buen Príncipe,» says the Emperor «no es mas / que un buen padre, el qual atento / debe cuidar de sus hijos: / y el Soberano que es bueno, / un hijo en cada vasallo / ha de mirar siempre» (act I). Wilkin describes the Emperor as «Aquella alma grande, aquel / magnánimo, justo y recto / corazon puede... no puede / hacer mas que lo perfecto» (act II).

Adelina is worried about the loss of her husband in battle. Derik, a loyal friend of the family, insists that a soldier, in order to maintain his honor, must risk everything in battle:

> El soldado valeroso,
> que respira un noble aliento,
> á quién sirve en ella? A Dios,
> al Rey y á la patria.
> ... El soldado que en la guerra
> no se expone a todo riesgo,
> es un vil, es un cobarde,
> é indigno de aquel acero
> que añade, y aun del honor
> que le dio su nacimiento   (act I).

The honor theme becomes dominant in the play when Wilkin, Adelina's husband, returns home early in the morning and finds the front door of his home open. He immediately fears the infidelity of his wife during his absence at war:

> Ah honor! quando las puertas
> que te guardan así advierto
> mucho peligro es el tuyo;
> ... Vamos, honor, y si alguna
> ofensa contra mí advierto,
> satisfaccion y venganza
> cruel, activa y fuerte ofrezco
> ... y dexe limpio y terso,
> purificados é ilustres
> mi honor, nombre y nacimiento;
> pues seria inmensa afrenta
> no siendo el castigo inmenso   (act I.).

What Wilkin does not know at this point is that Belfort, a wicked man who is an accomplice to the Baron de Tezel, a nobleman no longer in the favor of the court, entered his home earlier in the evening disguised as a sergeant to announce Wilkin's death in battle. He also left behind a letter stating that the Emperor abused his wife during his absence. All this was part of a plan to aid the Baron in the abduction and consequent seduction of Adelina.

Adelina feels offended that her husband would doubt her loyalty knowing the depth of her love and the rectitude of her character. Derik also feels offended since he was appointed to care for Adelina during Wilkin's absence. Derik is willing to take up his sword to prove Adelina's innocence: «sacad como yo el acero, / y dadme satisfaccion / de la ofensa que habeis hecho / á mi honor» (act II). All ends well when the Emperor, and thus Wilkin, discovers the Baron's perfidious scheme. The wicked characters are imprisoned, and Wilkin is made a captain for his heroic deed in battle.

Las vivanderas ilustres (1792) is probably Valladares' best drama in the lachrymose genre. It is an excellent example of the use of theater for the reformation of customs and the propagation of the «new» forms of morality. The play attacks the corruption and depravity of the nobility as well as unjust laws and edicts. It aims at moral reform by an arousal of feelings and sentiment. This elevation of feeling, found in passionate, frenetic gestures and embellished, emotional language, supplies the persuasive element. The drama is constructed in such a way as to keep the audience constantly in suspense, thus preventing their knowing the outcome until the last moment. Virtue does triumph in the end —«sabe Dios dexar premiada / la virtud» (act III)— as the wicked characters become upright, decent citizens and the joyous and content mood triumphs over the lugubrious and gloomy.

The attack on the nobility is found in two aspects of the plot. The Marqués de la Colina, acting irresponsibly, abandonned his lover Rosalia and their daughter Gertrudis several years ago, leaving them in an impoverished state. Rosalia expresses her censure of his moral turpitude:

> Nuestra infeliz situacion
> me aflige y causa tormento;
> no por la escasez de nuestra
> suerte contraria que llevo
> resignada, sino por
> el despotismo tremendo
> con que un poderoso logra
> avasallar al pequeño   (act I).

Rosalia, who has become a sutler to maintain herself and her daughter, lives in a state of «infelicidad eterna.» «Lloro, gimo y padezco,» she exclaims (act I).

The greater censure of this class in found in the Colonel's treatment of Gertrudis. The Colonel, son of the aforementioned Marquis, comes to inspect the troops and becomes enamoured of Gertrudis' beauty. He begins to bully and abuse her. Jacinto, her boy friend and one of the soldiers, comes to her aid as she yells for help. The nobleman's treatment of Jacinto in the following scene was clearly meant to stir the audience to action in order to bring about changes in certain customs and laws:

> COR.: Sabes quien soy?
>
> JAC.: Un soldado
> como yo no mas. No veo
> en vos otra insignia: os hallo
> violentando el honor terso
> de esta infeliz, que el amparo
> pide á un ultrage, y procedo
> como el Rey, y mi honor mandan,
> su claro honor defendiendo.
>
> COR.: Pues yo soy tu Coronel:
> me conoces?
>
> JAC.: Os respeto
> como á tal.

Cor.: Pues vete al punto.

Jac.: Usía deme el exemplo
retirándose.

Cor.: Te atreves
á disputar mi precepto?

Jac.: El honor así lo exige.

Cor.: Pues así enseñarte debo
á obedecerme.
Le da un bofeton.

Jac.: Y yo así
Saca el sable: embiste y el Coronel se defiende.
he de quedar satisfecho
de esta injuria.

Cor.: Temerario
qué intentas?

Jac.: Mi vituperio
lavar con tu propia sangre   (act I).

Jacinto is tied up and carried off. Before the court-martial of Jacinto is scheduled to begin, Gertrudis goes before the Colonel, pleading on hands and knees, for Jacinto's release. In a severe, pitiless and unsympathetic manner, he tells her to submit to his love or Jacinto awaits a vile execution. «Bárbaro, injusto, inhumano, / que abusas de esa manera / de tu sangre y nacimiento,» she reprehends sharply (act II).

In spite of the fact that one of the lieutenants testifies that Jacinto has always been an honorable and virtuous soldier, distinguishing himself on several occasions, the case is decided against Jacinto.[10]

The Marqués de la Colina, who has overseen the trial, feels great compassion for Jacinto. When he learns from Gertrudis, who now comes pleading to him for Jacinto's life, that Jacinto is innocent and was only defending his honor against the cruelty of his powerful enemy and, in addition, that his barbarous son tried to stain Gertrudis' honor, he laments the fact that the sentence has already been handed down. He feels that his son's crimes «son terribles producciones / que de mis culpas hereda!» (act II).

After learning that Gertrudis is his daughter, he goes before Rosalia to defend his desertion of her. Now that his wife, whom his parents made him marry, has died he will marry Rosalia.

The final setting corresponds to the somber, lugubrious mood of the action. The *chiaroscuro* of the dark forest, sparsely lit by the moon, with the sound of a somber march in the background corresponds to the agony of Gertrudis who stands before the supposed cadaver of Jacinto. (*Gertrudis... que vestirá luto, trayendo el pelo tendido, mal prendida, y haciendo fuertes extremos de dolor.*)

---

[10] The chief sergeant reads the statute concerning soldiers who offend their superior: «se le corte / la mano derecha, y muera / ahorcado para escarmiento» (act II).

Such a setting and scene would lead the reader to believe that the ending would be equally dismal, but following the predominant pattern, the dénouement is happy, and this contrast between one's expectation and the happy ending creates surprise, which in turn, always heightens emotion. The Colonel had given orders to save Jacinto and the King confirms his pardon. Gertrudis will marry her beloved.

If *Las vivanderas ilustres* is Valladares' best example of the genre, then *El carbonero de Londres* (1784?) is his worst. For this latter drama is an extreme example of a play whose only excuse for existing is found in the didactic speeches of its characters. These speeches have nothing whatsoever to do with the plot which, more complicated than most, is full of artificial devices.

Ricardo, the poor, but virtuous coal merchant becomes a spokesman for his class, and he moralizes on everything from the corruption of the cities and the decadence of the nobility to the merits of serving one's country in the army. The following speech is a typical example:

> La Corte ...
> ... es lo mismo
> que un Babel; porque se encuentra
> ninguna, ó poca verdad,
> habiendo infinitas lenguas.
> La tranquilidad alli
> no se conoce, pues reyna
> en todos sus moradores
> una confusion eterna.
> Y en efecto ...
> ... el mas
> alto talento no llega;
> porque hace la hipocresia
> que otras, con una apariencia,
> que la malicia dispone,
> se equivoquen con aquéllas.
> Y, en efecto, alli, Señor,
> la profusion, la opulencia,
> y el luxo se estiman; mas
> mi humilde trage desprecian   (act II).

Ricardo, with his «sensitive soul» and noble feelings, is guided by a sense of honor and dignity typical of all the virtuous characters in these *comedias lacrimosas*: «el que hace lo que / la humanidad nos enseña, / hace solo lo que debe» (act II). He embodies Rousseau's concept of «negative education» for he was raised in the mountains with no formal instruction. He is, therefore, «naturalmente discreto.»

The play has its dose of mystery and suspense with characters who escape to and return from the Indies, disguised personages, and even a beautiful young lady found alive in a buried chest. The three scenes of recognition add to the prevailing emotional tone. There is ample opportunity for

66

the audience to become involved with the characters who constantly assert their feelings and sentiments:

> Rusb.:
> ... A despecho
> de mi rubor, por los ojos
> copiosas lágrimas vierto   (act I).

> Isab.:
> lloraba, sin que pudiese
> mis lágrimas contenerlas   (act II).

> Gen.:
> ... á tu oído
> lleguen las cláusulas tristes,
> pero justas, los suspiros
> de mi amante corazon   (act III).

CHAPTER VII

COMELLA'S CONTRIBUTION TO THE *COMEDIA LACRIMOSA*

Among the seven *comedias lacrimosas* of Comella I should like to examine in this chapter, two present an exaltation of the middle-class, their
values and conventions, by developing the interaction of his class and the
nobility. *La Cecilia* (1786), a play reminiscent of *Peribáñez y el Comen-
dador de Ocaña,* exalts the sentiments and virtues of a poor, married woman
in contrast to the abuses and evil conduct of the Marquis, a dissolute and
corrupt young aristocrat, who falls in love with Cecilia at first sight.[1] Nevertheless, not only do we witness the wicked nobleman versus the honorable
burguesa, but also the enlightened aristocrat opposed to the depraved one.
The Count, father-in-law of the Marquis, is the very embodiment of an
eighteenth century enlightened nobleman. He is concerned with the well-
being of every citizen, and is a kind, prudent, generous man. He suggests
that his son-in-law give thanks to the villagers for the warm reception with
which they received him and his wife[2] by being charitable and humane:

> Repartiendo
> dotes á pobres doncellas:
> remediando con vestidos
> la injuria que la inclemencia
> causa al infeliz: franqueando
> á la viuda, que sus tierras,
> por pobre abandona, trigo
> para que á sembrarlas vuelva:
> socorriendo a los enfermos;
> dando limosnas secretas;
> y en fin, en quanto sea dable,
> remediando las miserias   (act I).

The play develops the eighteenth century notion, found in several of
these *comedias lacrimosas,* that nobility lies in deeds and not in titles. The
Count, in his condemnation of his son-in-law's behavior for attempting to

---

[1] This play may well be an adaptation of Charles Johnson's sentimental comedy
Caelia, or The Perjured Lover (1732).
[2] The play contains many lovely scenes of local color with dances and songs
which prepare the way for more elaborate scenes of this type in Romantic drama.

seduce Cecilia in her husband's absence discusses the real meaning of nobility:

> No eres tú noble: no lo eres:
> que la principal nobleza
> no estriba en executorias,
> ni en pomposas opulencias,
> sino en ser util á todos,
> ser de la Patria defensa,
> ser leal al Rey, y servir
> á Dios como Dios ordena:
> y el humilde que dirige
> sus pasos por estas sendas,
> es el verdadero noble;
> y al contrario, el que huye de ella
> se deshonra y envilece
> por mas noble que en sí sea: (act I).

The concept that nobility is transient and must be renewed is consistent with an age of rationalism and an epoch in which power shifts to the *bourgeoisie*.

The play, in its criticism of the nobility, in its spirit of dissatisfaction with existing social conditions,[3] in its concern for the individual and his sentiments, in its exaltation of virtue,[4] charity and humanity is a good example of the new morality which sentimental dramatists attempted to portray.

[3] In the Count's exaltation of country life in act I, a censure of existing social conditions is implicit:

> ¡Qué placenteros dias
> me dispensa el retiro de la Aldea!
> Entre sus caserías
> el alma noblemente se recrea,
> pues sin la cortesana desventura
> logra, haciendo dichosos, su ventura.
>
> Aquí de envidia exênto
> no codicia el deseo ageno empleo,
> ni ciego el pensamiento
> se dirige al lascivo devaneo,
> ni por razon de estado
> adora falsas lumbres el cuidado.
>
> Aquí naturaleza
> ofrece los objetos sin ficciones,
> honesta la belleza,
> la verdad pura, el zelo sin traiciones,
> llena el sol todo espacio;
> sin que á su luz se oponga alto Palacio.

[4] From the very beginning of the play virtue is extolled as the most important asset one can possess. Lucas responds to Cecilia's lament of their impoverished state with the following words: «...La felicidad / y la dicha verdadera / del hombre es conservar puros / el honor y la conciencia. / Estas máximas christianas, / que la virtud

The play's thesis is that virtue is the best way to correct vice:

> Y pues queda comprobado
> en este serio suceso
> que para enmendar el vicio
> es el mas prudente medio
> el medio de la virtud,
> dando al vicio buen exemplo.
> Todos: Sirva al soberbio de aviso
> y al humilde de consuelo   (act II).

This, of course, is purely sentimental. One must teach by example and not force. Virtuous behavior will instill more virtuous behavior. Feelings and sentiment, of which there are good examples in this play, become guides to truth and conduct. «Estas lágrimas que vierto,» says the Marquis to his wife, «hijas de la confusion / que ha introducido en mi pecho / la reprehension que tu padre / me dió esta mañana fiero» (act II). Cecilia, in a moving soliloquy, expresses her anguish and desire to instruct through an appeal to the heart: «Romped, suspiros mios, / romped aqueste pecho, / para que por mas bocas / respiren los pesares que padezco» (act II).

In the sequel, *Cecilia viuda* (1789), Lucas has died and Cecilia, impecunious, because the Marquis has reneged on his promise to give her a monetary gift as a token of repentance, is full of despair: «la tristeza que me cerca / es tan funesta, que verme / a mí misma no quisiera. / ... pues que de día y de noche / mi llanto y quejas no cesan» (act I).

Cecilia is pursued by two suitors, Don Fernando, a lieutenant and true friend who shares his salary with her, and Don Nicasio, the depraved administrador of the town. The latter takes advantage of his position to exercise his corrupt and evil ways: «¡Que vida tan placentera / es la mia! Todo el pueblo / á mi gusto se sujeta; / no respeto á la justicia, / defraudo todas las rentas, ...» (act I). Cecilia rejects these pursuers since she solemnly promised Lucas, before his death, never to remarry. Her primary concern is the maintenance of her honor. When Nicasio works his way into her home one evening, she takes a pistol and begs him to kill her, feeling her honor at stake. Fernando praises her virtue:

> Vuestra virtud, vuestro honor
> echaron tales cadenas
> á mi corazon sensible,
> que á los afectos que engendra
> el parentesco mas tierno
> el que os profeso supera   (act I).

pura enseña, / mas que el oro y fausto vano / sirven de alivio á mis penas» (act I). Another good example can be found in act I, when the Marchioness, jealous of her husband's interest in Cecilia, visits Cecilia to warn her of the Marquis' forthcoming arrival. Cecilia assures her she is virtuous and knows how to preserve her honor: «Nada importa; una alma noble, / aun en medio de las penas / sabe firme mantener / la constancia; siempre ilesa / tiene su virtud: ...Soy pobre, es verdad, soy pobre: / ¿mas qué importa que lo sea, / si sé conservar intactas / la virtud y la nobleza?»

Like its predecessor, the play has a strong social and moral orientation. Cecilia, in a speech to the Marquis in act I, criticizes the false pride and presumptuousness of the nobility:

> Señor, si entre los ricos hubiera
> menos presunción y mas
> sensibilidad, no fueran
> tan raros los hombres justos
> en el mundo.

Luis, a lad in the town, exalts the virtue of work. For him true nobility is found in hard work, rather than in the unproductive existence of the aristocratic classes:

> Mas honrado es quien gana
> el pan sudando
> que el honrado que vive
> del ocio esclavo.

The exaltation of work parallels the transfer of power from the aristocracy to the middle-class. While the old aristocracy's money was in land holdings, the new nobility, the *bourgeoisie,* had, among other things, labor to contribute.

In act II Fernando and Cecilia discuss the social obligation of a citizen. Cecilia is questioned by the justice of the peace about Nicasio's shooting at Fernando. Responding with a benevolent heart, she refuses to incriminate Nicasio: «El perdonar las injurias / al próximo, fuera de esto, / debe tener el Christiano / por gloria: de sus opuestos / debe ser amigo, y debe, / aun de su asesino mesmo, / besar la traidora mano, / y orar por su emienda al cielo.» Fernando, while appreciating her «corazón sensible,» feels her attitudes reflect a remissness of moral and social duty:

> Es verdad que es criminal
> la venganza en nuestros pechos,
> ... ...
> pero el daño que al comun
> resulta de los perversos,
> por medio de la justicia
> debe el ciudadano cuerdo
> precaver, porque mas vale
> separar del cuerpo un miembro
> podrido que no que dañe
> a todo el resto del cuerpo:

Once again we are presented with a work which works on the sentiments of the audience through moving scenes. *Cecilia viuda* is highly charged emotionally and tears flow freely. In a speech made near the end of the play by Fernando to the Marquis, Fernando expresses the grief he feels for Cecilia's death. Nicasio gave Cecilia poisoned water, believing she would reveal his perfidious acts. What Fernando did not know at the

71

time he made the speech was that the apothecary, suspecting Nicasio's treachery, prepared a benign narcotic instead of poison and that she will live.

> Conozco que me he excedido,
> mas no lo extrañeis, que es mucho
> el dolor que el cruel destino
> de Cecilia a mí me causa,
> y no teniendo otro arbitrio
> que el de llorarle; tormentos,
> penas, congojas, conflictos,
> conjuraos; y venid
> á afligir el pecho mio
> á porfia, para ver
> si de este modo consigo
> vengar su muerte llorando,
> ó dar fin á mis martirios.

Nicasio is killed on his flight to Portugal. Cecilia, remaining faithful to her vow to the end, plans to enter a convent. The Marquis, affirming that he has reformed his evil ways, promises to reward the good and punish the wicked:

> Y pues hemos visto, ya
> el fin que el vicio ha tenido,
> y que á la virtud la guarda
> Dios en el mayor peligro.
> Todos. Todos amen la virtud,
> todos detesten el vicio   (act III).

Los dos amigos (1790) is a play about friendship. Besides teaching a lesson in the true meaning of friendship, it develops the theme of the need of freedom for young people in the choice of spouses. Throughout the play craracters are giving advice to one another as to how they should behave. This drama is one of the least emotional examples we have in Spain.

Don Mariano is in love with a poor young lady named Doña Sinforosa. His father, who opposes his choice because of Sinforosa's social statuts, has selected an ugly, but rich mate for his son. Don Antonio, an inflexible, arrogant man, fails to recognize his son's charitable, sympathetic and tolerant nature. He accuses Mariano of squandering money when in reality he is helping humanity: «Padre mio, / no me aflijais mas el alma / con reconvenciones: / ... esta cierto / que en obsequio de la bella / humanidad dediqué / La mitad de la mesada / que me disteis» (act I).

Mariano's despair becomes even more pronounced when his dear friend, Don Jacinto, announces he will pay him a visit. Jacinto is anxious to share his newly inherited fortune with Mariano. Don Roque, an evil old man who is an acquaintance of Don Antonio and a friend and confidant of Sinforosa's aunt, Doña Nicolasa, has arranged for Jacinto to marry Sinforosa, thus alleviating the financial straits of Nicolasa. When Mariano takes

Jacinto to meet his girl friend all three realize their predicament. Mariano, in the spirit of friendship, renounces the woman he loves:

> ... Vinisteis,
> y hallo que el novio es mi amigo,
> y no amigo de estos tiempos,
> sino el amigo mas fino
> que ha ofrecido á la amistad
> los holocaustos mas dignos;
> en fin, que es otro yo, y siendo
> los dos en todo uno mismo,
> he resuelto renunciar
> á su favor mi cariño   (act II).

Sinforosa, while lamenting Mariano's abandonment, praises his extreme virtue: «Pues qué habia de ser de otra / aquel corazon tan fino, / tan virtuoso, que antepuso / á la amistad su amor mismo?» (act II).

In act III Jacinto, in a moving soliloquy, says he must place friendship before the dictates of his heart:

> Fuerza es irme, no hay remedio,
> ... ...
> mi amigo ama á Sinforosa,
> y yo ciegamente la amo.
> ... ...
> Porque mi amigo la quiere,
> porque es de él, porque he jurado
> morir por él, si es preciso,
> mil veces. Felíz Mariano,
> no temas que mi amistad
> te sea infiel.

Even though Jacinto has renounced his claim on Sinforosa, Mariano still has to contend with the unyielding character of his father. In act IV, Antonio is still stating his intention to arrange a *mariage de convenance*: «Yo le caso / con una cercana deuda / de un poderoso, que tiene / conexîones muy extrechas / en la Corte, que nos pueden / ventajosas consequencias / producir.» He declares he will disinherit his son if he disobeys him. Sinforosa, in her turn, must contend with the insensitive and unalterable nature of her aunt who insists she marry against her will. Sinforosa pleads that happiness in marriage depends upon desire and freedom in choice:

> considerad, que depende
> de la eleccion del estado
> la ventura ó desventura
> de los esposos ...
> ... No con tantos
> hijos que giman la fuerza
> de los padres inhumanos
> me confundais; y dexad
> que pueda sin embarazo
> usar del libre alvedrio
> de que el Señor me ha dotado   (act III).

The conclusion of this *comedia lacrimosa* is more successful and meaningful than those of Valladares which treat the same subject matter. In *Los dos amigos* the parents feelings are proved reprehensible and unjust and the virtuous characters' attitudes praiseworthy. There are no artificial devices, such as scenes of recognition, which affect the fate of the characters. Doña Nicolasa, upon learning that Mariano has been helping her and Sinforosa financially, asks Mariano how it is possible that she did not recognize his fine qualities earlier. Antonio, too, softens and is finally willing to bless his son's marriage to Sinforosa: «El dolor templa, / y vos dad á vuestro padre / los brazos: vuestra terneza / apruebo con bendiciones / repetidas» (act IV). Jacinto bestows one-half of his wealth upon the couple and leaves for Cádiz, happy that he was able to convince two headstrong, prejudiced elders that their children have a right to exercise their free will. Roque is punished in the sense that everyone recognizes what a scoundrel he is. The play ends with everyone praising: «Cómo debe / ser la amistad verdadera.»

El abuelo y la nieta (1778) discusses the topic of education and marriage. The subject of educational reform was a frequent topic in the later years of the eighteenth century in Spain.[5]

Comella's *comedia lacrimosa* is set in «una quinta de las inmediaciones de Madrid.» Two views of education are advocated. The grandfather, Don Diego, who has raised Doña Rosita since she was three, espouses Rousseau's general views on education.[6] In a speech directed to Don Benito, the well-to-do young man whom Diego has selected as the husband for his granddaughter, Diego explains how he stressed freedom, fresh air, country life, a moderate amount of study and lots of play in Rosita's upbringing and avoided the corruption of the cities and the evils of artificial politeness:

> ... Quando principia
> á desarrollarse el genio
> de los niños, se le oprimen
> con importunos maestros,
> que quieren con el castigo
> cultivar su entendimiento
> enseñandoles materias

---

[5] Two of Tomás de Iriarte's plays had as their subject matter the education of young people: *El señorito mimado* (composed in 1783 and first performed in 1788) and *La señorita malcriada* (written in 1788 and performed in 1791). Three of Leandro Fernández de Moratín's comedies also dealt with the topic of child-rearing: *El viejo y la niña* (1790), *El barón* (1787), and *El sí de las niñas* (1806).

[6] After 1750, Rousseau's ideas became known in Spain. The first important source for the dissemination of his ideas in Spain was Feijoo's refutation of Rousseau's first *Discours*, entitled «Impúgnase un temerario, que... en una Disertación pretendió probar ser mas favorable á la virtud la ignorancia que la ciencia.» (Carta XVIII of Vol. IV [1753] of *Cartas eruditas y curiosas*.) See Jefferson Rea Spell's book *Rousseau in the Spanish World Before 1833; A Study in Franco-Spanish Literary Relations* (Austin: The University of Texas Press, 1938). Pedro Montegón's two sentimental novels *Eusebio* (1786-87) and *Eudoxia, hija de Belisario* (1793) openly espoused Rousseau's ideas on education, the latter giving his views in regard to the education of women.

> tan estupidas como ellos,
> que sirven de hacerlos tontos,
> y criarlos entisecos.
> Yo me quité de etiquetas,
> tontunas y cumplimientos:
> apenas cumplió tres años,
> mandé que comiera aquello
> que quisiese; ...
> Igualmente mandé al aya;
> que en verano, y en invierno,
> fuese á la hora que se fuese,
> saliese á la huerta en cuerpo,
> sin resguardarla del sol,
> ni del rigor de los yelos.
> Que si la tomase embrazos,
> algun pastor ó quintero,
> y la llevase á la siega,
> ó al prado á ver los corderos,
> no la pusiesen reparo;
> y aunque volvia de entre ellos,
> apestando á ajos y á vino,
> manchado todo el pañuelo,
> y el vaquerito arrugado
> y lo regañaba al verlo,
> en el modo de reñirlo
> conocian mi contento.
> En fin, con estas anchuras,
> poca labor, mucho juego,
> un estudio moderado,
> y quatro mimos á tiempo,
> he criado una muchacha,
> mas rolliza que un ternero,
> que me dará, si se casa,
> á porrillo los viznietos   (act I).

On the other hand, Don Josef, her father, is appalled at her unpolished, inelegant manners. When she greets him, he criticizes her decorum:

> Quanto á besarmela vuelvas,
> te has de poner de rodillas:
> lo entiendes? Y porque sepas
> que ni la edad, ni el empleo
> de esta obligacion dispensan
> á los hijos, tu descuido
> corrijo de esta manera   (act II).

He wants her to go to Madrid to learn proper conduct and etiquette: «Soy un padre que desea / ver su hija correjida» (act III).

Applauding Rosita's natural ways, Benito tells Josef that the very notions he (Josef) holds have contributed to the break-down of familes:

> ... y el luxô
> que en las Europeas reyna,

75

amortiguó los afectos
que engendra naturaleza
en las mugeres que fundan
su ambicion en ser caseras;
me hizo ver palpablemente
que muy pocas de ellas piensan,
que deben sus diversiones
ser su familia; ...
Este descuido que muestran
á sus deberes, y el ansia
que en dexarse ver emplean,
... que vendrá dia,
que el decoro, la modestia,
la fe conyugal del sexô,
tendrá que huir á las selvas,

... ...

Esta pintura infeliz,

... ...

de la corrupcion que reyna
en las costumbres, no tiene
en vuestra hija trascendencia   (act II).

The theme of choosing one's mate is secondary in this play. Don Diego, completely out of keeping with the liberal ideas he espouses in child-rearing, has chosen Benito as a husband for Rosita. It is contradictory for a man who advocates Rousseau's subjective expression not to allow his granddaughter to exercise her free will and choose a husband of her liking. Her father also supports her union with Benito because, although he collects a large salary, he cannot pay off his debts unless his daughter marries a wealthy man. Rosita expresses her hostility towards these attitudes in a speech to her governess:[7] «Con el novio? / Sabe usted si yo le quiero?» (act I). Doña Mónica replies, echoing the elder's conservative views: «Aquello que hagan sus Padres, / deberá usted dar por hecho.»

---

[7] In a very melodramatic speech in act II, Rosita again describes how abhorrent the idea of marriage with Benito is for her:

Como me caso
contra mi gusto,
será el disgusto
fruto de amor.
Sentir,
penar,
gemir,
llorar,
es lo menor
que he de pasar.
Mis pucheritos,
mis suspiritos,
mis lagrimitas,
empapaditas,
en este lienzo,
puedes mirar.

The play also criticizes the Catholic Church by ridiculing the *abbé* and through him the overpopulated ranks of the clergy, large numbers of whom had no proper religious function to play. The *abate* was the object of incessant satire in eighteenth century Spain.[8] Since he had no real function to perform in the church, he often earned a living as a tutor in well-to-do families. He was a favorite in feminine circles but could not marry. Often he played the role of confidant and go-btween. They were generally attired in elegant dress and were considered authorities on the latest styles.

Don Pedro, the *abbé* in *El abuelo y la nieta,* is a musician. He is a ladies' man, causing Rosita to fall in love with him and even suggesting marriage with him. He functions as an intermediary, giving Benito advice as to how he can gain Rosita's affection. He discusses food and fashion, elaborating on the styles of the petimetres. Although supposedly a religious man, he is intolerant:

> PEDRO:
>
> > Qué escandalo! Qué maldad!
> > con un negro unas doncellas?
> > Sabeis que es un negro?
>
> JUAN:
>
> > [a black lackey of Don Josef] Un hombre
> > como tú, y como qualquiera.
>
> PEDRO:
>
> > ... pero se forman
> > del pos de naturaleza,
> > Y así, á esclavos de blancos,
> > el destino los condena   (act III).

It is difficult to fit this play into the genre because it does not develop any sympathy for any particular character and therefore it is impossible to ascertain whether Comella applauds the more natural Rousseauesque notion of child-rearing or the rigid, formal method supported by the father. Rosita asks for her father's forgiveness at the end of the play, saying that she will attend a school of correction and thus be worthy of Benito's affection. It is a *comedia lacrimosa,* not because of the attitudes it has towards the middle-class, but simply because it does discuss them.

Natalia y Carolina and *El hijo reconocido* deal with the abuse of authority in the parent-child relationship. *Natalia y Carolina* (1789) has no dramatic impact or validity except as a tract on the aforesaid relationship. All of these plays should have been sociologic tracts. The play is quite credible on the thematic level; the father repents, cries and finally allows his daughter to exercise her will. His evil ways are not rewarded. But on the level of the plot, the drama is very contrived with its mysterious incidents, its disguised characters, its various scenes of recognition, etc.

---

[8] See for example Torres Villarroel's first «Visión» of the Third Part of his *Visiones y visitas de Torres con don Francisco de Quevedo por la corte* and Ramón de la Cruz's sainetes entitled *La presumida burlada* and *El fandango de candil.*

The drama presents the tribulations of Natalia, a young woman who has run away from her parents' home in Holland because of their harsh and oppressive nature: «Bien pudieras conocerlo: / para huir de la violencia / del mas tirano precepto» (act I). In a boarding house in Bordeaux, she lives a life of utter despair disguised as a boy named Milton. She had been in love with a certain young man named Aleman, but her father refused to grant her permission to marry him. Her life is complicated by the fact that Carolina, a young lady in Bordeaux, falls in love with her. Carolina suffers deeply when Milton tells her marriage is an impossibility. In one of the many emotional scenes in the play, Carolina describes her anguish:

> Todo ha sido sentimiento,
> zozobra, inquietud y angustia
> para mi sensible pecho;
> ... ...
> vivo solamente para
> mi amado Milton, muriendo
> sin poder morir, y sin
> llegar a vivir viviendo.
> Dolor acerbo!
> ¡Que tormento!

Aleman, who also left Amsterdam and by coincidence came to Bordeaux to avoid seeing Natalia married to another, has fallen in love with Carolina and proposes marriage. She rejects him because of her love for Milton. Full of jealousy, Aleman challenges Milton to a duel. As Aleman is about to shoot, he recognizes Milton to be Natalia. After a tender embrace, in a moving scene of recognition, Natalia tells the story of how she fled and came to France. She speaks of the persecution suffered at the hands of her father and her yearning for liberty.

In act II, Natalia, feeling victimized and rejected by everyone, expresses her grief.[9] She learns that her father, Enrique Sumers, has arrived in Bordeaux as a Dutch consul. Sumers, ashamed and full of remorse, attempts to locate his daughter. In a speech which exemplifies a basic tenet of sentimental comedy, namely, that moral reform cannot be effected from without, at the dictate of force or authority, but rather from within (the spirit must be first aroused, and then guided by the feelings), Sumers declares that in spite of his tenacity his heart has taken over:

> Soy padre, sí, y la terneza
> á pesar de mi tesón
> del corazon se apodera.
> Dexad, señor, que en tributo
> ofrezca á naturaleza
> estas lágrimas; dexad
> que espíe por medio de ellas

---

[9] «¿Contra una infeliz muger / pueden combinarse á un tiempo / mas desgracias?... / Todo, todo me amenaza: / mi Padre, mis sentimientos, / Carolina... De una vez / huyamos de estos funestos / sitios.»

> una culpa que Natalia
> cometió por mi entereza;
> ... ...
> de mi excesivo rigor
> dimanan todas mis penas;
> abusé de mi poder,
> quise que Natalia fuera
> víctima de mi precepto.

Natalia receives a letter stating her father's desire to pardon her and marry her to Aleman. The proprietor of the boarding house, whose tone is didactic throughout the play, sums up the thesis:

> Hé aquí padres obstinados
> las funestas consecuencias
> de vuestra severidad?
> si no quereis probar de ellas...
> Todos. La inclinacion de los hijos
> consultad con la prudencia.

Carolina, learning the true identity of Milton, finally finds relief from her despair.

El hijo reconocido (1799) is consistent with Diderot's ideas on sentimental comedy in that it deals with family relations. The play, very moral in tone throughout, is a reworking of the theme of the return of the prodigal son. It involves the relationship between a father, son and grandson in an upper middle-class home in Cádiz: «Salón con dos puertas laterales: Gavinete en el foro con bufete y sillas; sillas decentes repartidas por la escena; encima de una de ellas habrá un sombrero y un baston; aparece don Matías almorzando.»

The initial scene contains many realistic touches with its discussions of food and everyday customs. Don Pedro expresses to his father Don Matías his extreme satisfaction with his new employee named Martín. Indeed he plans to give this young man a share of the business, his wealth when he dies, and even the woman he has chosen to be his son's wife. Feeling disgraced by his son Josef, Pedro has disowned him: «Es insufrible / ...las suyas [faltas] no pueden tener enmienda» (act I). Throughout the play Pedro voices the disgust and contempt he holds for his son. (These attitudes are indeed extreme for a father to have towards a son whose only failing was that he was a spendthrift.) Matías defends his grandson on the grounds that he is young and that Pedro was also a wild fellow as a youth: «todos fuimos calaveras; / debe antes mirar sus faltas / el que juzgue las agenas» (act I). Martín informs Matías that he is really his grandson. While José laments his father's implacable nature,

> Qué esperanzas tener puedo
> en vista de su dureza!
> su rencor es implacable,
> de nada sirve la enmienda:
> de nada?   (act I).

79

he feels he must prove his worth to Pedro before making his identity known. The action is brought to a head when Matías tells his son that José is about to arrive for a visit. «Sea reo, ó no lo sea,» says Matías, «has de estrecharle en tu seno» (act II). Pedro looks for a sword. (This is really outrageous.) Nevertheless, once Pedro realizes that Martín is, in fact, his son he embraces him, cries for joy and declares: «Todo me parece un sueño: / que en Martín encuentro a Pepe, / y en un mal hijo uno bueno!» (act II).

The thesis, as stated by Don Pedro, is that an extravagant, corrupt person can become a good, responsible being:

> Vamos pues. El jóven loco,
> que ha perdido su concepto
> con su estragada conducta,
> para cobrarle de nuevo
> procure seguir los pasos,
> procure tomar ejemplo
> del Hijo Reconocido;
> pues ha demostrado al pueblo,
> que si quiere el hombre malo,
> puede pasar á ser bueno.

Indeed, it is Don Pedro, whose attitudes are contemptible, who will have to follow the exemplary behavior of his son. Don Josef is an example of a hero who represents a mixture of virtue and vice depending upon whose viewpoint is being supported. He is the son of a man whose values are odious. Pedro hated his son when he was a spendthrift, and loves him when he is not.

The play is a nullity. It is not a plea for tolerance. It is not even a good polemic. Ostensibly these *comedias lacrimosas* propound to be social plays, but usually they fail. They are slaves to the prejudices of the epoch in which they were written. Their only saving grace is that they probably were an impetus towards social reform.

La buena nuera (1794) differs from Comella's other *comedias lacrimosas* examined in this chapter. It does not contain any social commentary; its subject matter is neither the theme of marriage, nor parental abuse; neither friendship, nor education. But it is a sentimental, lachrymose comedy in the respect that it treats middle-class citizens and puts its faith in the innate goodness of man and consequently tries to affect his conduct by appealing to his emotions. The plot is more complicated than those of most *comedias urbanas* and makes use of artificial devices, such as scenes of recognition, to bring about the happy *dénouement*.

Cosme feels hatred and vengeance towards his daughter-in-law Jacinta because he feels she is responsible for the death of his son Olaguer. Jacinta, completely distraught, recounts the story of his son's death, insisting that Olaguer fell off a precipice into the sea. Cosme insists that she threw him into the sea, justifying his reasoning by stating that Jacinta married Olaguer against her will. She resents the injustice of his accusations: «Mi suerte está decidida; / vuestro rigor me condena, / no mi crimen» (act I).

She begs for his blessing: «ved que os lo ruego llorando; / ...Dadme vuestra bendicion / que la espero de rodillas; / no me negueis una gracia / que la inocencia os suplica» (act I). Cosme, with tears in his eyes, is truely moved. He embraces her, pardons her and begins to call her daughter:

> O tu ficcion es muy grande,
> ó la virtud te apadrina.
> ... á pesar de mis enojos
> á perdonarte me obligan;
> me conducen á abrazarte
> y hacen que te llame hija.

An official from the High Court of Barcelona arrives looking for Jacinta. The Court has decreed her death. Nevertheless, the new mayor of the town, Don Bernardo, takes pity on Jacinta. He wants proof that she is a criminal: «Yo no quiero / que á ninguno se le oprima / sin fundamento / ... Infeliz mujer! Dios sabe / que su suerte me lastima» (act I). His judicious attitudes in regard to the law are paralleled in his enlightened plans for the town which include the encouragement of labor and industry, the opening up of uncultivated lands, the proper lighting of streets and the building of a house of charity. In all walks of life he aims at progress.

Jacinta's sorrow and adversity make her think of suicide. She plans to liberate her daughter and father-in-law by sacrificing her life:[10]

> ... yo no puedo
> soportar mas una vida
> tan penosa: mi desgracia
> me abandona á la ignominia
> del suplicio ...
> padre, hija, á libertaros
> voy á costa de mi vida   (act I).

When Jacinta appears before the mayor she assures him of her innocence. While he is extremely compassionate and sympathetic to her plight, he cannot free her before a trial. Bernardo, who recognizes Cosme as someone he knew in Mexico, frees Cosme and gives him money to help take care of his granddaughter. Bernardo is the very embodiment of the «personnage sensible» glorified in sentimental comedy with his tolerant, humane and charitable character.

An actual trial takes place in act III. While Bernardo is convinced of Jacinta's innocence, he finds no proof to offer as evidence. Jacinta is once again feeling rejected and persecuted when an unexpected turn in events brings about a happy *dénouement*. Olaguer returns home bringing a sealed letter with him.

---

[10] The notions of sacrifice, redemption and martyrdom are frequently found in the *comedia lacrimosa* as they will be in Romantic drama.

6

OLAGUER.

> Quien me despierta?
> padre, sois vos?

COSME.

> El mismo es.
> Hijo!

OLAGUER.

> Padre!

The letter reveals that Bernardo, abducted as a small child, is also Cosme's son. Olaguer confirms Jacinta's story of his fall explaining how he was captured by pirates and taken to Argel «donde he vivido llorando / mi libertad y mi ausencia / por quatro años» (act III). He proceeds to have an emotional encounter with his wife and child. The virtuous characters have been rewarded, «Pues triunfó / del engaño la inocencia» (act III).

The seven plays of Comella studied in this chapter exemplify the themes and techniques of the *comedia lacrimosa*. Viewed as a single entity they support the thesis of this study that this genre was part of the eighteenth-century's thrust towards rationalism, humanism, and democracy or, more broadly, towards attitudes and beliefs that would support the aspirations of the middle-class against those classes (the nobility); those institutions (the church); those conventions (arranged marriages); and those attitudes (the glorification of wealth and station as opposed to honest labor) that would subjugate them.

Chapter VIII

ZAVALA Y ZAMORA'S *COMEDIAS LLORONAS*

Don Gaspar Zavala y Zamora was the most prolific writer of *comedias lacrimosas*. The techniques he employed and the themes he developed were identical to those of the other Spanish dramatists already discussed. His most popular subject was the censure of the Spanish custom of marriage through parental imposition, but he also dealt with the topic of the unfaithful husband and the virtuous wife; the subject of honor and the evils of jealousy; the theme of friendship and the abuse of authority in the parent-child relationship. Most of the plays can be characterized as melodramas since they are developed sensationally with little regard for convincing motivation and with a constant appeal to the emotions of the audience. The characters are always types with the struggle being between the good and the bad. The plays are didactic and in some cases the thesis is taken up and discussed pro and con in the manner of argumentation and debate.

The term *melodrama* literally means a play with music, and in two of Zavala's works songs, recitative and choruses, aid in the development of the dramatic action. *El amor dichoso* (1790?) is such an example. The *mise en scène* is pastoral rather than urban and contains numerous realistic details which provide local color. The pastoral names of the characters and the type of versification employed correspond to the rustic mood.

As the play begins the mood is one of joy and contentment. The scene is full of sunlight, and Dantéo, a poor, young farmer sings of the glories of nature in a buoyant *romance*. The magnificence of the scene surrounding him reiterates the beauty of his feelings:

> Quán apacible y hermosa
> la mañana está! Qué fresco
> vientecillo corre! Y quánto
> nos hace mas alhagüeño
> y grato el sitio el susurro
> blando que forma moviendo
> continuamente las hojas
> de esos arboles! Qué bello
> presentan ahora á la vista este
> monte, los reflexos
> que le presta el sol!

83

But when he considers his predicament; namely, that Patricio, a wealthy stock farmer, refuses to marry his daughter Belisa to him because he considers Dantéo beneath his social station, his mood and vision of nature change abruptly:[1]

> Mas no viene, y yo no vivo:
> no llega, y yo no sosiego.
> Pero qué mucho, si el valle
> sombrio está, está funesto
> sin su vista: si esos campos
> que ostentaban otro tiempo
> su lozanía, están mustios
> porque no la ven: y en fin,
> si ese blanco álamo bello
> que la arrulló tantas veces,
> con el blando y lisongero
> rumor de sus hojas, hoy
> parece que está suspenso,
> porque Belisa no viene   (act I).

Thinking only of his own interests, Patricio has arranged for Belisa to marry Delio: «es rico, es noble, y del Pueblo / la mejor estampa» (act I), not caring at all about Delio's dubious character.

Dantéo's anguish is accentuated by the lugubrious music heard in the background. «*Cae traspasado de dolor en el poyo de piedra: Música triste, con la qual va poco á poco volviendo de su abatimiento*» then «*Suspendiéndose arrebatado, mientras tocan dos compases de música fuerte.*» He takes out a knife, «*y durante la música, escribe en el tronco del álamo, interrumpiendo este acto con algunos suspiros, lágrimas y extremos, la siguiente octava.*» A chorus emphasizes and underscores the tragic tone:

> Coro:
> Ya aquí se acerca
> desconsolada:
> qué desgraciada
> la hizo su amor!   (act I).

Next we have a *cavatina* followed by Belisa's *recitativo* where she expresses her dejection and grief in words reminiscent of Garcilaso's Sonnet X:

> Triste Belisa,
> adónde tu pesar, dónde tu ciega
> pasion te guia? Acaso
> piensas hallar aquí la dulce prenda
> por ti llorada? En vano
> la llama tu dolor y desvarío.
> Ni la selva, ni el prado
> ni los ásperos montes, ni los troncos
> te dirán de ella ya   (act I).

---

[1] This is just one of several examples of a phenomenon known as «egocentric pantheism» found in the *comedia lacrimosa*. The notion that there is a rapport between man and nature; that nature becomes a confidant and is in accord with man's sentiments, will be fundamental in Romantic drama.

Again we hear the sound of «una marcha lúgubre» followed by «música agitada» and a chorus which sings «Gemid, gemid, amigos. / llorad todos, llorad» (act II).

The gloomy, lugubrious tone changes to one of joy at the very end when it is discovered that Dantéo is the son of a gentleman and has inherited a large estate. It is only then that Patricio is willing to toast the lovers.

The play is supposed to be a censure of the pride and prejudices of established society. But it fails just as *El trapero de Madrid and Rufino y Aniceta* of Valladares failed. The selfish, prejudiced attitudes of Patricio, rather than virtue, are rewarded.

El amor perseguido y la virtud triunfante (1792) is similar in mood and theme to *El amor dichoso*. It is set in «una Quinta cerca de Manzanares» with various shepherds and shepherdesses cutting wood, milking goats, feeding cattle and picking fruits. The time is early morning; the initial mood is again happy and festive. But the dolorous quickly takes hold and prevails as Benita is told by her uncle Pasqual, majordomo of the estate, that he forbids her marriage to Jacinto, a poor shepherd. Jacinto, too, describes his malaise and melancholy in a speech typical of the Romantic *mal du siècle*. He describes the suffering, emptiness, abandonment and loneliness that he is experiencing. He is a victim of «la risa universal,» like Tediato in Cadalso's *Noches lúgubres*:

> Porque está esperando
> con ansia, aquel dulce instante
> postrero, de este cansado
> aliento mio: aborrezco
> estos momentos infaustos
> de vida que gozo, y solo
> mi pena, y continuo llanto
> son en esta soledad,
> los compañeros mas gratos
> á mi mal.

For him suffering gives pleasure:

> ... qué llanto
> tan feliz! ¡Oh que suspiros
> tan dulces!   (act I).

Within the framework of a plot which treats the theme of arranged marriages, many social and moral issues are examined. There is a glorification of virtue, as the most praiseworthy quality one can possess. Benita defends Jacinto's admirable character to her uncle:

> Amo la virtud, la fé,
> la honestidad de Jacinto;
> nació pobre, sí; mas fuera
> un horroroso delito,
> que por buscar intereses,
> olvidara requisitos
> tan apreciables   (act I).

Jacinto defends virtue as an end in itself:

> Señor Pasqual, yo imagino,
> que el amor casto y honesto,
> no vive, como habeis dicho,
> de caudales; la virtud
> le mantiene, y en sí mismo
> encuentra su recompensa   (act I).

Patricio, the righteous owner of the estate, condemns Pasqual's attitudes: «...que si un pobre es virtuoso, / sale al instante, del baxo / estado en que esta, y se eleva / su virtud» (act II).

The play contains a defense of the poor man and his worth to society:

> JAC.:
> Señor Pasqual, vedlo claro:
> en el comercio del mundo,
> vende el pobre al rico el grano,
> que en premio de sus fatigas,
> le produgeron los campos:
> vende el rico al pobre, el oro
> que con tantos sobresaltos
> adquirió: luego en substancia,
> el pobre, es tan necesario
> al rico, como este al pobre,
> y aun mas, si bien lo notamos,
> porque el rico, sólo es rico
> por el pobre, y este alcanzo,
> que no necesita al rico,
> para ser pobre   (act II).

This is just another example of the type of speech found in these sentimental comedies to apotheosize the middle-class. These plays were the mouthpiece of the revolutionary *burgeoisie* and always reflected their values.

We also find a condemnation of the evils of society found in city life and a commentary on the true meaning of nobility. Patricio tells Benita that:

> ... La hidalguia
> nunca la dan los honores
> y puestos á que sublima
> la suerte al hombre ...
> ... ...
> Su nobleza
> durará, mientras le asista
> su fortuna. Pero aquel
> á quien sus virtudes dignas,
> su juicio y su providad
> ennoblecieron un dia,
> aunque le falte la suerte
> su nobleza se eterniza.
> ... en la Corte

> Adulan muchos, y pocos,
> por lo regular, estiman
> la verdad, quando se opone
> á sus maxîmas iniquas.
> ... Y, finalmente, es la Corte
> una habitacion continua
> de la confusion, el luxo,
> la profusion, y la envidia   (act III).

For the Pre-Romantic writers there was a direct relationship between the simple, honest man, living in modest middle-class circumstances and the «innocence of nature.»

As in all melodramas and sentimental comedies poetic justice is secured, the characters being rewarded or punished according to their deeds. Enrique and Pascual's evil ways are discovered when they attempt to abduct Benita; they repent. Pascual gives his permission for Benita to marry Jacinto. The play ends with these lines spoken by Patricio:

> ... pues se mira
> que *el amor perseguido,*
> y á pesar de la malicia
> la Virtud triunfante.

Zavala y Zamora uses the world of finance and commerce as a background for *El perfecto amigo* (1790) and *El triunfo del amor y la amistad, Jenwal y Faustina*[2] (1793) but never enters into the detailed economic discussions that Valladares did in a few of his sentimental comedies. The set of *El triunfo del amor,* the most popular of Zamora's sentimental comedies, promises the development of a plot dealing with such matters but this is not the case: «La accion pasa en Bristol. La escena es en un departamento de la casa de Darmont, en que habrá dos bufetes con escribanías, libros de caja, algunos legajos de correspondencia, una pequeña mesa de juego y buena sillería.» The plot is just another story of a poor apprentice in love with a wealthy merchant's daughter. It is very similar to Valladares' *El trapero de Madrid.* In both plays the well-to-do father is ruined financially and the husband he has chosen for his daughter refuses to assist him. It is the poor apprentice who redeems him financially, and only then is his praiseworthy character recognized.

Darmont is unfaithful to his own ideals. He tells Faustina, his daughter, that «La virtud es la verdadera nobleza, la verdadera riqueza, la verdadera sabiduría. Sé virtuosa, y todo lo serás en el mundo» (act I, scene ii). But his conduct is prejudiced and bigoted, insisting that Faustina marry a wealthy (and insipid) man.

Vangrey, the chosen beau, has one redeeming feature. He is so absurd that he adds a note of humor to an otherwise dry, tedious, prosaic play. He demonstrates his superficial knowledge using lofty, swelling language

[2] This play was based on Lillo's *The London Merchant.*

and quoting famous people and books, often in Latin. He is particularly fond of examples taken from Greek mythology. Turning down another drink offered by Darmont, he exclaims: «No quiero mas: he bebido ya dos copas, y me expongo á que me llamen Tricongio, como al Emperador Tiberio, si bebo la tercera» (act II, scene ii). His pedantry is most evident in the scenes with Enriqueta, Faustina's maid. Enriqueta is a delightful character, quick-witted and clever. It is she who tells Darmont what an inane man Vangrey is: «un estafermo fastidioso, que la [Faustina] esté moliendo con latines y mas latines, enamorándola en griego, y halagandola en hebreo» (act I, scene v).

Jenwal is the ever-faithful lover who must endure the hardships of injustice and prejudice and remain tolerant, generous, tender and humane through it all.

In *El perfecto amigo* (1790), also known as (*Los*) *viajes de José II*, Ricardo, a miller, has to choose between marrying his fifteen-year-old, daughter Eduarda to his nasty, seventy-two-year-old, parsimonious creditor Distoorn, in order to save himself financially, or allow Eduarda to marry the poor worker Enrique, whom she loves, and lose his cabin and mill by incurring the wrath of Distoorn.

Ricardo believes his daughter is entitled to marry whomever she chooses. He represents the «new morality» founded on the natural goodness of man; he is tolerant and humane. Although poor, Ricardo is more concerned with the happiness and well-being of his daughter than the preservation of his limited worldly goods. Honor for him means dignity and not reputation, as it does for Don Basilio, Patricio, Darmont and the plethora of fathers in these *comedias lacrimosas*. He is generous in his reception of Joseph II, Emperor of Germany, who is passing through his village disguised as a traveler. In spite of his poverty, he receives this stranger with great hospitality.[3] Joseph rewards him by marrying his daughter to Enrique, while giving them all a handsome monetary gift.

Esmit, a farmer, is «el perfecto amigo.» The theme of friendship was frequently developed in this genre. Friendship was viewed as one of the major keys to goodness in the world. Esmit plans to sell his material goods and give the proceeds to Ricardo so that he can pay off his debt to Distorn. When Enrique is drafted Esmit insists upon going to war in his place so that Enrique can be near his widowed mother and sweetheart.

El bueno y el mal amigo[4] (1790?) is another play about friendship. The topic of friendship was particularly appropriate to this genre since it reflected the new Shaftesburian or Rousseaunian concern for one's fellow man. Now instead of the love of God, we find the love of humanity. When God was no longer the sole source of man's consolation there was a new bond between man and man, just as there was between man and nature. This is one of the most melodramatic of the so-called *comedias nuevas,* with characters who are either very virtuous or extremely evil; with the

---

[3] In this respect the play is reminiscent of Lope's *El villano en su rincón.*
[4] This play was modeled after Edward Moore's *The Gamester.*

constant use of tears to effect changes of conduct; with *tableaux à la Greuze* and with an exclamatory style, characteristic of the emotional tone of the work.

The plot deals with another somber aspect of domestic life; namely, an unfaithful husband and a virtuous wife. Quintina expresses her grief about Leonardo's irresponsible and unfaithful behavior. Even though she must suffer and endure constant humiliation and abuse, including begging in the streets to maintain her five year old son who is dying of hunger, she is always gentle, loving and full of compassion towards her husband:

> ... Dí, por qué lloras?
> no turbes el regocijo
> de mi alma. Habla, qué tienes?
> qué suspiras dueño mio?
> no tiembles: entre mis brazos
> estas: respira tranquilo.
> ... Te amo tanto:::   (act II).

Leonardo, though full of vice, is basically good at heart. He is influenced by two friends. Don Anselmo is the virtuous, devoted, charitable friend who, although angered by Leonardo's bad habits and inconsiderate treatment of his wife and child, cannot resist helping him. Claudio is the unfaithful, deceitful «friend» who leads Leonardo astray into drinking, gambling and having romantic affairs. He plays on Leonardo's sympathy to entice him to return to the arms of his mistress:

> CLAUD:
> Ella llora, ella suspira
> ella grita; vaya, creo
> que si no vas pronto allá
> pierde el juicio.
> LEON:
> Alma,
> con este dolor no puedo   (act I).

In the final act Leonardo learns a final lesson in the meaning of friendship. Two constables arrive at his home to seize his belongings since he cannot pay his creditors. In spite of the fact that Leonardo was generous with Claudino, Claudino refuses to assist him. Anselmo bails him out.

> LEON:
> A los dos suplíca
> mi amistad que me ayudeis
> á celebrar esta dicha,
> comiendo conmigo: y pues
> tenemos hoy á la vista,
> lo que un buen amigo sirve,
> y lo que el malo arruina.
> TODOS:
> Despierte la juventud
> dócil, incauta y sencilla   (act III).

El amante generoso (1790?) is another good example of this minor and transitional genre with its serious treatment of middle-class problems (financial matters, censure of the nobility, theme of choosing one's mate, topic of dueling); its didactic and moral orientation; and the use it makes of sentiment.

Consider the opening scene where Christina, a young Swedish girl in love with her cousin During, a Swedish military official, expresses her despair:

> *Christina sentada en una silla de brazos, reclinando sobre la mano la mejilla, y como manifestando su situacion el abatimiento de su espiritu.*
>
>> Corazon, ¿quándo podrás
>> latir con algun descanso?
>
> *Se levanta, se acerca á mirar el Relox, y dice lánguidamente:*
>
>> Las cinco no mas. ¡A el que una
>> ventura aguarda, qué tardo
>> le parece que anda el tiempo!
>> Y á el que la está disfrutando,
>> qué veloz! Hasta las seis,
>> corazon mio, volvamos
>> tú á tu agitacion, y yo
>> á mi dolor y mi llanto   (atc I, scene i).

This is yet another of those plays where the father only consents to marry his daughter to the partner of her choice when he discovers he is rich and can be of some use to him. Up to the moment that Parliament declares During to be the legitimate owner of the estate which Daerts took away from him at his father's death, Daerts' treatment of his daughter and nephew is harsh in the extreme. He warns Christina that he will kill her if she refuses to obey his wishes to marry Kerson, of noble birth:

>> Y tú vil hija, prevente,
>> á obedecer mi mandato,
>> ó á ser víctima agradable
>> de este puñal, y esta mano   (act I, scene xix).

Christina is doomed to suffer. She bemoans the fact that a being as sensitive as she («mi sensible corazon» act I, scene ii), must experience loneliness, abandonment, rejection and despair.

During, «el amante generoso,» must endure not only the indignities of Daerts but also of Kerson. Kerson, knowing of Christina's love for During, challenges During to a duel to cleanse his honor:

>> Los que nacieron
>> nobles como yo, no sufren
>> que haya labio tan grosero,
>> que se atreva á denigrar
>> su puro honor con dicterios.
>> Vos During, me habéis tratado: :
>> Y á satisfacer vengo: : :
>> Matandoos   (act II, scene iii).

During, knowing that dueling is against the law,

> ¿Y sabeis que prohibidos
> están por el Rey los duelos?

opposes the match. He tells Kerson to select more noble means to keep his honor in tact:

> Tratar siempre
> verdad: obrar con mas seso:
> pensar con nobleza: en fin
> ser virtuoso: (act II, scene iii).

During finally agrees to the match when Kerson calls him a coward. When Kerson is lying on the ground he announces the esteem he has for During.

The play is a failure. While supposedly teaching us a lesson as to the true meaning of nobility, it rewards, instead, egotistical, prejudiced behavior.

El amante honrado (1775?) proposes to exhibit the evils of jealousy. This play shows that it is possible for a mistaken idea to be repeated often enough, through circumstance and slander, to produce the situation suggested. The play is similar in theme and technique to Echegaray's El gran Galeoto with its duels; its melodramatic and sensational effects; and its grandiloquent style.

A series of incidents occur to confirm Arnil's belief that his wife Sidney is unfaithful. Believing that she is still in love with her old boy-friend Falclan, and thus feeling his honor at stake, he leaves. He loses all his worldly goods because a law suit is not decided in his favor.

Sidney continues to be faithful and loving toward Arnil: « ¡Ay honor! toda mi vida / seguiré tus leyes» (act I). She is the typical virtuous heroine of these sentimental comedies who exhibits all the noble human ideals.[5] Her kindness toward her supposedly poor cousin Varnil pays off. Once Varnil discovers how generous Sidney is, with the little she has, he reveals that he is extremely wealthy and will bestow his entire estate on her. Arnil finally decides to return to his wife but feels ashamed to do so because of his financial straits. Falclan, «el amante honrado, another of those generous and faithful friends who remain loyal whatever the cost may be, pays off all of Arnil's debts and Sidney praises his benevolent nature:

> Oh corazon, el mas noble
> y generoso de quantos
> celebra el tiempo, pues no
> me permite ya mi estado
> recompensar las finezas
> que os debo: :   (act III).

Las víctimas del amor, Ana y Sindhám (1788) differs from all other comedias lacrimosas in one important respect. It is the only example of the

---

[5] «Yo he nacido / sensible,» says Sidney «y no puedo / dexar de atender al grito / de la pobreza» (act II).

genre in Spain in which fortune does not move from bad to good, but rather from bad to worse.[6] Such a play helped destroy the tradition that only the misfortunes of the great are of tragic interest. In all other respects it is a typical sentimental representation of contemporary life with its highly-wrought emotional scenes, its advocation of a morality based on humanity, tolerance (Baron de Fronsvill) and friendship (Mauricio), its cult of the feelings[7]

ANA:
mas solo un suspiro
de Sindhám, una ternura,
un sentimiento nacido
de su amante corazon,
recompensa estos martirios   (act II),

its glorification of sincerity and purity in the state of nature as compared to the evils and corruptness of the cities and its censure of the nobility.

Ana, daughter of Milor Darambi and wife of Sindhám, servant of the same lord, must hide the fact that she has been married for ten years because of her father's extreme disapproval of Sindhám, due to his lower social class. The play proposes to be a sermon against such injustice. Sindhám expresses this iniquity to his wife:

él admitiria un yerno
noble y rico, aunque tuviera
los mas enormes defectos:
yo soy pobre y soy humilde:
tu corazon, bien diverso
del de tu padre, no quiso
sacrificarse indiscreto,
al poder y la riqueza;
miraste con menosprecio
esos dones, en que el mundo
funda los merecimientos
del hombre, y amaste á un pobre   (act I).

Milor Darambi has arranged for Ana to marry the Baron de Fronsvill. The Baron, whose attitudes about marriage are completely different from those of Darambi, represents the enlightened man of the eighteenth century:

...Mucho la quiero,
es verdad; pero si ella
admite aqueste himeneo,

[6] English playwrights differentiated between sentimental comedy and domestic tragedy on the basis of the dénouement. In domestic tragedy the protagonists were overcome by adverse occurrences which were out of their control. In sentimental comedy they were finally rewarded for moral behavior.

[7] ZAVALA Y ZAMORA, in the «Advertencia al lector,» in the 1797 edition of the play, stated: «He procurado proponer diversos caracteres de nobleza, de virtud... Su regular entable, sus sentimientos, el contraste de pasiones vehementes y la ternura del asunto son interesantes.»

> con repugnancia, es error,
> que yo insista. No pretendo
> sacrificar á mi gusto
> su corazon...
> ... Mas antes
> la casara yo, os confieso,
> con un pobre virtuoso,
> que con un rico soberbio   (act I).

He elaborates on his ideas in act III: «... Las Damas / nacen libres, y sería / una injusticia obligarlas / á amar á quien las estima. / ...y nunca / obrar con tal tirania / pudo la naturaleza.» Milor Darambi embodies the conservative, established viewpoint:

> Yo no tengo
> dominio sobre su gusto;
> como padre, le poseo
> sobre su persona;   (act I).

Such a predicament leaves Ana and Sindhám doomed. Ana lives in a estate of constant despair: «lo que mas lloro y siento / es, que no tengo esperanza / de que mejoren los cielos / nuestra suerte» (act I). She curses her destiny:

> Ana infeliz, en qué dia
> tan horrible y tan funesto
> naciste! Qué negro instante,
> aquel, que mis ojos vieron
> á Sindhám

Sindhám finds death as the only solution to his *fastidio universal*:

> ... En diez años
> no ví dia sin martirio
> noche sin desasosiego,
> noche sin grande peligro,
> ni instante sin sobresalto,
> y por fin hoy, se han unido
> todos á afligirme ...
> ... Ah, Sindhám triste,
> qué lexos está el alivio
> de tus penas! ...
> ... la vida, la aborrezco;
> dexame morir!   (act II).

Milord finds out about Ana's clandestine marriage and comes to pursue her with dagger in hand. Ana, Sindhám and Pamela, their daughter, appeal to him, in a moving *tableau,* to change his harsh stand: (*Sale Sindhám, Pamela y Ana, y los dos primeros se arrodillan á los pies de Milord, que quedará suspendido.*)

ANA:

> ...los tres sumisos
> vuestro poder imploramos,
> señor, rogando hoy activos
> vuestros pies, con nuestro llanto:
> concededlo compasivo,
> padre, ...

PAMELA:

> Si, señor, perdone usted
> á mis padres, abuelito.
> Míreles con qué amargura
> llorando están. Yo me aflijo
> tambien de verles.

SIND:

> Ea, señor, si el recuerdo
> del duro oprobio que vino
> por Sindhám á vuestra casa,
> os hace no oir los gritos
> del amor y la ternura,
> aquí está mi pecho, heridlo,
> y redima con mi sangre
> la afrenta que os origino   (act II).

While their speeches arouse pity in the audience, Milor, totally unmoved, puts his everlasting curse on them. His change of heart comes too late. Finally convinced by the Baron that his treatment has been cruel, savage and pitiless he begs forgiveness. Sindhám has fallen from a tree and died and Ana has decided to take her own life.

El naufragio feliz (1782) is not didactic, nor does it present middle-class problems. But, like Comella's *La buena nuera,* it is a sentimental comedy with its profuse emotional expression, with its *tableaux* and moving scenes of recognition. It is completely manipulative to make people cry. The play is also an excellent precursor for Romantic drama.

The drama, being set on an isolated island off the coast of Coromandel, is suggestive of the sentimental exoticism of Chateaubriand of twenty years later, a theme which will be discussed in the final chapter. Timante, an English businessman who came to India to gain his fortune, and his nephew Cleodon were shipwrecked five months before. Archima, the supposed daughter of Tucapél, chief of the Indians, arrives at their site and falls in love with Cleodon. As she goes in search of a safe dwelling to hide these Englishmen, she leaves behind a memorandum book. Timante examines the book which relates the misfortunes of his wife, whose whereabouts he did not know. Reading that she was pregnant when he sent her on a journey, he realizes that Archima is his daughter. Cleodon is captured by the Indians. Timante tells Archima that she is his daughter and begs her to find a way to free Cleodon:

> ...implora
> la piedad de esos perversos,

94

> vierte lágrimas, emplea
> las gracias que te dió el cielo,
> en ablandar sus feroces
> corazones   (act II).

ARCH:

> iré a implorar la piedad
> de mi padre: el llanto tierno
> de su hija, ablandará
> su corazon, y : : :

Gómel, one of the principal Indians, frees Cleodon and wants to be given Archima's hand in marriage as a reward. In the meantime Timante, alone, hears some shots and sees two men appear in a launch. One of the men is Agenor, beloved father of Cleodon. The following scenes, produced by the physical arrangement of the actors, were to work on the sentiments of the audience. The development of action through gesture and movement was to enhance the sentimental force of the play and produce «une émotion douce.»

> *Hechandose Agenor precipitadamente en los brazos de Timante.*

AGEN.:

> Que reparo.
> Timante.

TIM.:

> ...Oh Dios! Agenor.
> ...Ay Agenor!

> *dexandose caer en sus brazos traspasado de dolor. Al ir á partir por la izquierda salen Cleodon con todo el cabello suelto y Archima: Agenor al verle se arroja precipitadamente á sus brazos, y Timante á los de Archima.*

AGEN.:

> Hijo amado.

CLEO.:

> Padre. Buen Dios.

The final words are spoken by Gomél who, once kind and tender, is now cruel and vindictive because Archima has rejected him. As Archima and her newly found family are about to flee in a launch, Gomél tells her that she will find a venemous knife awaiting her.

Eduardo y Federica (1811) is an excellent example of the genre and an important prototype for Romantic drama with its mysterious incidents and scenes of recognition; its impassioned, eloquent language; its use of prose; its lugubrious, gloomy elements which correspond to the action; its heroes who are both virtuous and sinful simultaneously, depending upon the viewpoint society takes on them; and its heroine's feeling of despair, abandonment, solitude, rejection and malaise —the Romantic *mal du siècle*— and her yearning for death.

It is clearly a bourgeois drama and takes place in an upper middle-class home in the environs of London. The themes which are presented and discussed are the very problems which concerned this class: the right to choose one's own mate in marriage; the cruelty of «public opinion»; the tyrannical behavior of parents and the ensuing crises. This latter theme, also developed in Comella's *Natalia y Carolina,* was frequently presented in literary works in the final years of the eighteenth century.

The play is didactic in tone and ethical in nature. The thesis is to show the tragic consequences of parents who are oppressive and inflexible in their relationship with their children. Milord Derikson's severe, uncompromising character causes his daughter Federica to run away from home and when in need of help, because her lover abandonned her, refusing to confide in her father:

> Mi mal! ah! mi mal! No puede ser comunicado. La muerte debe sepultarle para siempre! ... No padre mio: vivirá esta infeliz oprimida de trabajos: la despedazarán el dolor y el remordimiento; acabará sus dias en los montes abandonada del cielo y de los hombres: pero no tendreis jamas que avergonzaros de su culpa!   (act I).

Milord Donbay, to whose house the languid Federica is brought, is the sympathetic, compassionate, tender antithesis of his friend Derikson. This «black and white» treatment of characters, with no shadings to their personality, is typical of this genre. The following incident, which is central to the plot, demonstrates their different positions. Eduardo has told his father that he is guilty of a dreadful wrongdoing. «Pues no me ocultes nada,» replies Donbay. «Soy tu padre, y te ayudaré á remediar el daño» (act II). When Eduardo reveals that he wronged an innocent girl, his father tells Derikson that he wants his son to marry this aggrieved young lady and not the one he had originally chosen for him: «Hoy... tiene la grandeza de decirme voluntariamente su culpa, y quiere pagar su deuda: ¿qué mas honrado hubiera sido en este caso Derikson?» (act II). Derikson suggests that if she is of a lower social class they could give her money as compensation for his offense, thus maintaining appearances. Donbay retorts:

> El oro jamás curó la opinion llagada.
> Solo sé que las leyes de la providad no
> dan ni quitan la gravedad á la culpa por
> respeto á la calidad del reo, ni aumentan
> ó disminuyen la satisfaccion á proporcion
> de la clase del quejoso. Todos los
> culpados son iguales á sus ojos, y todos
> los agraviados son igualmente atendidos.

DERIKSON:

> Y por respeto á esas leyes, ¿será bien que
> se envilezca tu linaje?

MILORD:

> El crimen es el que envilece al hombre; ...
> No, Derkison: jamás creeré ofender mi noble
> generacion por hacer esposa de mi hijo, á
> una joven honesta y virtuosa, aunque no sea
> de elevada estirpe ... estoy determinado
> á dejar bien puesta la reputacion de esta
> joven, casandola con mi hijo   (act II).

Donbay embodies the Pre-Romantic idea that society, in order to be just, must be concerned with the individual and his feelings, rather than with its traditional norms and prejudices. True virtue and nobility only rest in a society where sympathy and benevolence prevail. Donbay expresses this concept to his son: «El verdadero mérito del hombre, no está en haber nacido noble por acaso, sino en hacerse noble por medio de sus virtudes. Una mala accion basta á perder la reputacion del hombre, y mil acciones buenas, no bastan después á recobrarla» (act II). Donbay is the type of individual who elevates humanity by exemplifying and encouraging noble conduct.

At the end of the play, Derikson receives a letter from Federica, whom he had thought dead, begging forgiveness. It is only then that he learns the consequences of his domineering behavior. Milord Donbay, while giving Derikson a reply as to why his daughter never came to seek his help, sums up the moral:

> He aquí el funesto resultado de la excesiva severidad de algunos padres: se hacen temer de sus hijos; estos los tienen por inflexibles, y en vez de confiarles sus desgracias para que puedan repararlas, se las ocultan con cuidado, haciéndolas así irreparables, ó cayendo de unas en otras por callar las primeras.

Such a theme lends itself to the lachrymose genre. Feelings, sentiments and emotions are given free reign in the play, and an exclamatory style, characterized by leaders, exclamation marks and periphrasis, is prevalent throughout.

CHAPTER IX

A THROWBACK: GIL Y ZÁRATE'S

CECILIA LA CIEGUECITA

Antonio Gil y Zárate is best known for his historic dramas. But he also wrote tragedies, *comedias de costumbres* in the manner of Leandro Fernández de Moratín and a lachrymose comedy entitled *Cecilia la cieguecita* (1843).[1]

This play is a very late example of this minor genre. It presents the theme of the right to choose one's partner in marriage. The middle-class is the center of concern and while the play does not have a thesis *per se*, the new ethics asserted in all sentimental comedies are stressed. Feelings and passions are freely expressed and there is plenty of opportunity for the shedding of tears.[2]

The play is set in Madrid in the year 1840 in the elegantly adorned home of Don Juan, a successful lawyer. Juan exemplifies the most noble human ideals; «siempre con piadosos fines» (act I, scene i). He is sensitive, kind, charitable and tolerant. Juan has just returned from France, bringing with him the orphan daughter of a friend. He falls in love with Clotilde and proposes marriage. She agrees saying that she owes him her

---

[1] There is no relationship between this *comedia lacrimosa* and Comella's *La Cecilia,* or *Cecilia, viuda.*

[2] Clotilde's soliloquy, the opening speech in act II, is one of the best examples found in all of sentimental comedy. In this monologue she expresses her anguish at the thought of marrying Juan, her benevolent guardian:

> Llorad, llorad, ojos mios,
> y no dejeis de llorar:
> ya que logro sola estar,
> derramad el llanto á rios
> á impulsos de mi pesar;
> y en tan acerbo dolor,
> pensando en el bien que adoro,
> pues la suerte con rigor
> me veda tan tierno amor,
> déjeme exhalarle en lloro.

life. «Jamas consentiré yo / seas por fuerza mi esposa,» says Juan. «Quiero una prueba amorosa, / un sacrificio, eso no» (act I, scene v).

Juan is loving and generous with a poor blind musician he meets. Truely moved by Cecilia's unfortunate life story («Esas lágrimas me prueban / tu bien corazon» —act I, scene viii)—, he offers to become the benefactor of this young lady and her brother.

When Juan learns that Clotilde has run off with another man, he plans to take his life. He is saved by Cecilia, who professes her love and compassion for him:

> Y pronto á participar
> de vuestra pena y quebranto,
> pronto con vos á llorar,
> aceptando sin pesar
> la mitad de vuestro llanto   (act III, scene x).

Cecilia la cieguecita, written several years after the most popular Spanish Romantic dramas, has many thematic, philosophic and technical characteristics in common with Romantic drama. It is a drama of action and not of characterization. The characters are always types. The play is very fast moving with specific times mentioned frequently which add to the time pressure experienced during the drama. Not only does the drama present the emotionalism and sentimentalism typical of the *comedia lacrimosa,* but also the most outrageous extremes of melodrama, typical of Romanic drama. Enrique's pretended suicide to convince Clotilde to run away with him is such an example. The language is declamatory; the gestures, passionate and frenetic; the style, impassioned. Practically all moralizing is absent from this play as it is from Romantic theater. Juan and Cecilia are beings with sensitive hearts and superior souls who experience the malaise and wearisomeness typical of the Romantic *Weltschmerz.* They feel alone, abandonned, rejected, bitter, victims of «la risa universal» of Cadalso's Tediato:

CECILIA:

> Y ¿á mí
> que me importa el mundo, qué?
> ¿Qué tiene con ese mundo
> la pobre ciega que hacer?
> Me despreciarán, con mofa
> me señalarán tal vez,
> se reirán de mí . . . En buen hora;
> rian, muestren su desden:
> por fortuna ni su risa,
> ni su mofa puedo ver   (act II, scene xv).

JUAN:

> Ya. ¿qué me queda? Morir,
> morir solo. ¿Qué me importa
> la vida, si es un tormento
> cada dia, cada hora;
> si entre pesares contínuos

ha de ser triste, afanosa;
si una mano en este mundo
no encuentro consoladora
que mis lágrimas enjugue,
que me apoye en mis congojas;
si solo mis beneficios
ingratos, traidores forman;
y en fin, si llevo grabada
en mi frente la deshonra,
debiendo ser de las gentes
desde hoy mas escarnio y mofa?   (act III, scene ix).

This «fastidio universal» leads to suicide, a frequent solution to man's grief in Romantic drama.

Sí, sí, mas vale morir
... Pero ¿qué veo?
¡Cielo santo, unas pistolas!
... Pues el beneficio acepto;
y una bala matadora
dé en este momento mismo
á este infeliz muerte pronta
... ...
... me abruma
el peso de la existencia;
y es fuerza acabe la suma
de mis males con violencia,
ó que el tedio me consuma.
... justicia no hay en lo humano
y es la libertad mentira.
Abrir mi pecho al amor
por último consentí;
y ahora que con dolor
cifro mi vida en su ardor,
el amor huye de mí   (act III, scene x).

The theme of salvation, martyrdom and redemption is fundamental in this play, as it is in Romantic drama. Every Romantic hero views himself as a redeemer and savior. While the religious and biblical symbolism found in plays such as *La conjuración de Venezia, El trovador, Don Álvaro o la fuerza del sino* and *Don Juan Tenorio* is not as abundant, it does exist.

CECILIA:
Vos, Clotilde, y yo, debemos
sacrificarnos por él;
y mayor gloria tendremos
si el sacrificio es cruel (act II, scene ii).

Clotilde describes her projected martyrdom:

Sacrificarme debo.
Y ¿lo podré yo hacer ...? Pues qué, ¿no llevo

> de esta pasion frenética, invencible,
> aqui clavada la punzante flecha?
> Mis ojos la dirian: sonrojado,
> mi semblante do quier la declarara,
> y en lágrimas desecha,
> arrastrada sin vida al pie del ara   (act II, scene ix).

Cecilia saves Juan and longs for the peace and innocence of Eden:

> cual dos espíritus puros
> que ante el Soberano Ser
> sus angélicos amores
> gozan allá en el Eden   (act II, scene xv).

The fact that such a play was written in 1843 proves that the tradition of the *comedia lacrimosa* remained alive throughout the period of the Romantic drama, which it influenced.

CHAPTER X

THE *COMEDIA LACRIMOSA*

A PRECURSOR OF SPANISH ROMANTIC DRAMA

The Romantic cosmology in Spain was first evident in the early 1770's in works such as Cadalso's anacreontic «A la muerte de Filis,» published in *Ocios de mi juventud* in 1773; Cadalso's *Noches lúgubres* (1771-1774); Meléndez Valdés' ode «A la mañana en mi desamparo y orfandad,» (1777); and his second *Elegía moral* entitled «A Jovino, el melancólico» (1794). From *El delincuente honrado* (1773), the *comedia lacrimosa* was in the same Pre-Romantic tradition.

In spite of all its defects, the *comedia lacrimosa* had one redeeming feature. The ideas and techniques it set forth provided the initial stimulus for Romantic drama. Romanticism represents the freeing of feeling, instinct and sentiment in opposition to reasoned objectivity. All of these elements (which are foreshadowings of the Romantic subjection of the world to the self) found voice and sanction in the *comedia lacrimosa*.

Several Spanish Romantic critics noted the influence of sentimental comedy on Romantic drama. Jerónimo Borao, in his article «El romanticismo» in the *Revista Española de Ambos Mundos,* 1854, II, pages 801-842, notes that «La Chaussée elevó a sistema estos tibios matices del futuro romanticismo y creó la comedia lacrimosa que Diderot vino a modificar.» [1] In addition, he affirmed that «la tragedia moderna [romántica]... va a buscar el placer y el dolor a los abismos del corazón; ... en el suntuoso hogar doméstico» (p. 163), a concept clearly derivative of sentimental comedy or domestic tragedy. Finally, while speaking of the etimology of the word *Romantic,* Borao again emphasizes the relationship with the sentimental genre: «Su etimología nos indica el punto de donde viene: *romanesco, romancesco* y *romántico* expresan todo lo que se parece a la novela, lo que se presenta con aire extraño, lo que afecta de un modo enérgico a la imaginación ... lo que ofrece sentimientos excéntricos. ... En este sentido, dice Moratín de la comedia *Salvaje* que es una obra romancesca, y Ville-

---

[1] Reproduced by Ricardo Navas-Ruiz, *El romanticismo español: Documentos* (Madrid: Ediciones Anaya, 1971), p. 151.

main dice lo propio de algún personaje de Destouches y de la manera general de La Chaussée.» [2] Leandro Fernández de Moratín had already related the word *romancesco* with «el género cómico lúgubre» while discussing the tragedy *Douglas* by John Home.[3]

Luigi Monteggia spoke of tears in Romantic plots in his article «Romanticismo,» published in *El Europeo,* 1823, I, pp. 48-56; «Cuando los argumentos románticos ... son manejados por un verdadero poeta, ¿quién es el hombre que no se halle arrebatado al verlos representar? Las virtudes y los delitos, las dichas y las desgracias, nos recuerdan las circunstancias de nuestra vida y hasta los clasicistas no pueden contener las lágrimas, entre tanto que con las palabras critican el uso de tales argumentos, que forman la delicia de los románticos» (Navas-Ruiz, 37). The notion that the moral power of tragedy was more effective representing everyday, ordinary life was, of course, the basis of sentimental comedy.

Ramón López Soler, speaking of the essence of tragedy in Romantic drama in «Análisis de la cuestión agitada entre románticos y clasicistas,» *El Europeo,* 1823, I, pp. 207-14 and 254-59, pointed out that the means used to produce pity and compassion in the audience were the same as those employed in the *comedia lacrimosa*: «Si ,en lugar de irritar a nuestros nervios procura ablandarlos por medio de cuadros más delicados y melancólicos; si se propone excitar en nosotros sentimientos de amor, de suavidad y de ternura, presentándonos situaciones patéticas en las que más lleguen a interesarnos los delirios y la profunda tristeza del alma que los furiosos arrebatos del cuerpo, probaremos cierto placer en el interés que nos cause y derramaremos tal vez lágrimas dulcísimas de sublime compasión» (Navas-Ruiz, 45).

Before concluding this study with an examination of how certain thematic, philosophic, and technical characteristics of the *comedia lacrimosa* anticipated Romantic drama, it is necessary to establish clearly that we are dealing with two very distinct elements. The *comedia lacrimosa* is a minor genre; Romantic drama in Spain is a part of the whole phenomenon of Romanticism which is reflected in philosophy, the arts, the social sciences and institutions of the central elemental thrust of the modern age. All criticism now in existence has yet to get a definitional handle on the Romantic movement as a whole, but during its course, (which has, perhaps, finally been run), man redefined his relationship not only to nature and God, but to any element of law or custom that stood between his desires and their fulfillment. While the implications behind this statement suggest questions at the center of intellectual inquiry, this study will conclude with a focus on a mere splinter of the issue. In relating the *comedia lacrimosa* to Romantic drama in Spain, one must concentrate on a single element: the transition from the utilization of the senses to an appreciation of the sensory experience. The progression from the *comedia lacrimosa* to Romantic drama

[2] RICARDO NAVAS-RUIZ, *op. cit.,* pp. 155-56.
[3] See his *Obras póstumas* (Madrid: Imprenta y Estereotipia de M. Rivadeneyra, 1868), III, p. 186.

cannot be linked to any ordered philosophic outlook brought to bear on artistic expression, but rather to a discovery that it feels good to feel.[4]

In dealing individually with each of the plays that I have identified as lachrymose comedies, a few seemed to have no purpose at all other than to make the audience cry. It is in these plays that we can begin to mark the transition to Romantic drama where the preoccupation is no longer with ameliorating social conditions, but with feelings.

What characterizes the difference of the role of sensibility in the eyes of sentimental dramatists from those of Romantic drama is that the former propose a clearly moral goal: they claim they can correct vice by means of sentiment. Practically all moralizing is absent from Romantic drama. To put it another way, one tradition tried to use art to promote ideas, the other, to promote feelings and emotions that had no other aim other than the production of similar feelings and emotions in the audience.

Romantic drama in Spain will continue to rely heavily upon sentiment because sentiment induces feelings—or more importantly, sensuous experience which feels good. The ultimate areas of a critical understanding of what I am describing are probably physiologic, but introspection leads us to realize that emotion results in putting us in touch with ourselves.

The Romantic artist looked at nature in a particular way not because the philosophy of sensationalism explained to him how knowledge was acquired, but because by assisting him to engage his senses with what is out there (nature), it enabled him to feel a certain way. The Romantic poet and the naturalist are very distinct in their roles, even if the way they start viewing nature is similar. The Romantic artist who views a blade of grass so minutely as to discover the pulse of photosynthesis, and subsequently moves quickly to the pulse of nature, assimilating it into his own pulse, is quite simply getting a «high»; one could anticipate the march towards drugs to induce similar feelings. Indeed, all the progression which this chapter traces from sentiment to sensuality and frenzy, found in Spanish Romantic drama, are logical extensions of an art centering ever more on feeling and sensation.

I will now give several examples from Spanish Romantic dramas showing

---

[4] My approach here is purposefully crude and invites comparison to that used by Russell P. Sebold in «Enlightenment Philosophy and the Emergence of Spanish Romanticism,» in *The Ibero-American Enlightenment* (Urbana: University of Illinois Press, 1971), where the philosophy of Locke and specifically his *Essay on Human Understanding* are put forth as having a major influence on the origins of Romantic poetry in Spain. I am most comfortable with Professor Sebold's assertion at its end that «individual philosophers are less important as influences that shaped Romanticism than as illustrations of the larger inductivist pattern of the European mentality that shaped philosophy, literature, and all the other arts from the eighteenth century on» (p. 139), If there is any heresy left in the 1970's in the world of scholarship and criticism, it is probably the belief that since there is a great deal that is neither quantifiable, much less provable, one might as well be provocative. Although much of this study has concerned itself with identifying similar cultural and philosophic influences on writers whose plays are studied herein, my predilection for explaining literary characteristics in terms of subjective discovery, as opposed to the more identifiable influences, is merely because I tend to think of the artist alone in his garret, rather than exposed to the academies, other artists, official boards of censorship and all other elements making him responsive to things other than his impulse to create.

the heightened and highly emotional response among the characters to events, actions and sentiments. Since the body of this book shows such examples in sentimental comedy, there will be no need to repeat them here.

I. FROM SENTIMENTALISM TO SENSUALITY AND FRENZY

La conjuración de Venecia still relies heavily upon sentiment and emotion to arouse pity. Indeed, Martínez de la Rosa, in his *Apuntes sobre el drama histórico,* published in 1834 in conjunction with the aforementioned drama, stated that sentiment and emotion are the elements which have real impact on the audience: «me parece necesario tratar ante todas cosas de *conmover el corazón,* presentando al vivo *sentimientos naturales* y lucha de pasiones, que ése es el mejor medio, si es que no el único, de embargar la atención, de excitar interés, y de ganar como por fuerza el ánimo de los espectadores» (the italics are mine).

Laura, wife of Rugiero, looks to the Virgin Mary as a possible source of consolation for her anguish: «*(Dirígese con el mayor abatimiento hacia la capilla y se arrodilla delante de la verja.)* Tú eres mi solo consuelo, protectora de los desdichados; tú ves con piedad estas lágrimas que corren de mis ojos ... Yo no tengo más madre que tú ... Pero si hemos merecido, por nuestra triste unión, el castigo del cielo; si somos los únicos en la tierra que no alcancen con el llanto su perdón y misericordia ..., caigan sobre mí, sobre mí sola, cuantos males puedan amenazarnos ... Hasta las lágrimas son dulces, madre mía, cuando se derraman en tu seno ...» (act II, scene ii).

This play still uses emotion as a means of persuasion. Having revealed her secret marriage to Rugiero to her father, Laura pleads for her father's help. He is moved by her supplication: «Desahoga tu pecho, hija mía ...; cualesquiera que sean tus desgracias, si tu padre no puede remediarlas, las llorará contigo ... ¿Qué más quieres de mí? ... *(Laura se levanta y se arroja en brazos de su padre.)* Más vale así, más vale que llores ... ¿No sientes consuelo, hija mía, en llorar en el seno de tu padre?...» (act III, scene ii). Juan Morosini, in turn, plays on the emotions of his brother Pedro, president of the Tribunal, to get Rugiero freed: « ¡Estoy pensando que no tienes hijos ... Y que no vas a comprenderme! ... Es que nunca me he visto en la afliccion de hoy... *(Enjúgase una lágrima de los ojos)* [5]... Laura es ya de Rugiero... Rugiero ha desaparecido desde anoche; y tú sabes de cierto

---

[5] The Romantic notion that the shedding of a single tear indicated a grief much more profound than the shedding of many is also found in *Alfredo.* Alfredo describes the spirit that has summoned him to go forth in search of his father, missing for fifteen years: «pero la sombra se levantaba silenciosa en el fondo de mi aposento: dos lágrimas corrían por sus tristes mejillas» (act I, scene i). In scene iv, of the same act, a pilgrim comes to see Alfredo who is going to the Holy Land. He explains that the troubador, from whom he learned the ballad he is singing, «solia correr una lágrima por sus mejillas,» when he sang out the name of Ricardo. More examples can be found in the Romantic novels *Sancho Saldaña* by Espronceda and *El Doncel de Don Enrique el doliente* by Mariano José de Larra.

dónde está... ¿Cómo has de comprender mi dolor, si no tienes hijos?...
Pero recuerda que tuviste uno; y que pudiste hallarte en el mismo caso
que yo ... También yo te he visto llorar ...» (act III, scene iii).

Macías by Larra is an exceedingly sentimental drama. Elvira cries day
and night over her misfortune. Macías has not returned in the time alloted
by her father, and she will be made to marry a man abhorrent to her:

> *(Elvira echa una ojeada de dolor a Beatriz, que desaparece lentamente:*
> *se levanta y queda apoyada con una mano en el sillón y enjugándose*
> *con la otra las lágrimas, que trata de reprimir con un esfuerzo violento).*

> ... ahogando mi dolor durante el día,
> que mis lágrimas tristes, por la noche,
> en el oculto lecho derramadas,
> entre la soledad y las tinieblas
> pasión tan grande, que olvidar no logro,
> en eterno silencio confundiesen.
> Mas, ¡ay!, que no está en mí. Ya, mal mi grado
> rompe mi lloro, en mi dolor inmenso,
> el dique que hasta aquí lo ha sujetado   (act I, scene iv).

Macías, alone in the tower where he is imprisoned, bemoans his state:

> *(Después de un momento de pausa, sumergido en el mayor dolor y ena-*
> *genación).*

> ¿Así al más rendido amador se trata?
> ¿Cupo en tal belleza tanta alevosía?
> ¿Qué se hizo tu amor? ¿Fué todo falsía?
> ... ...
> ¡Oh! ¡Lloren mis ojos! ¡Lloren noche y día!

> *(Queda un momento abismado en su dolor)*   (act IV, scene ii).

An excellent example of the use of tears to effect change is found in
act V, scene iv of *Alfredo*. When Ricardo returns, Berta begs him to have
pity on her and her transgressions: «¿Me perdonareis? ¡Oh! no me levantaré! ¡no me levantaré de vuestras plantas!... Dejad que las bañe con mi
llanto de la gratitud y del consuelo!... ¡Ah! Puesto que vos me perdonais...
puesto que las lágrimas que corren por mi pecho han podido enternecer
vuestra alma...»

A similar scene is found in *El trovador* when Leonor begs mercy for
Manrique to the Count.

> LEONOR: *(Arrodillándose.)*
> ¡Ah!, conde, conde, piedad.
> ... ...
> ¿No os apiada mi dolor?

NUÑO:

> ¡Apiadarme! Más y más
> me irrita, Leonor, tu lloro,
> que por él vertiendo estás   (act V, scene v).

Leonor declares that «yo para llorar nací,» in act I, scene iii.

El paje (1837) is still excessively sentimental. Ferrando and his mother, with whom he is passionately in love, cry throughout the play.

FERRANDO:

> Madre tierna, madre mia,
> Si vieras á tu Ferrando,
> Al hijo de tu alegría
> Llorando en la noche y dia   (act I, scene vi).

FERRANDO:

> ... ¡Tus ojos vierten
> Llanto de compasion! ... ¡Dichoso el hombre
> Que del llanto de un ángel es la causa!
> Dime, dime señora: ¡tú de amores
> Lloraste alguna vez? ¡Ay! ¡cuan terrible
> Es amar en silencio, alimentarse
> De lágrimas ardientes, ver la vida
> Entre amargos ensueños deslizarse!   (act III, scene viii).

Another play which uses emotion as a tool is *Los amantes de Teruel* (1837). In the later Romantic plays, such as *Doña Mencía* (1838), *Alfonso el Casto* (1841), *Simón Bocanegra* (1843), *Don Juan Tenorio* (1844) and *Juan Lorenzo* (1865), while sentiments are asserted and feelings expressed, emotions are more reserved, controlled and restrained than in earlier works.

In act II, scene iii of Hartzenbusch's play entitled *Los amantes de Teruel*, Isabel tries to convince her mother of her father's oppresive attitudes. Apart, she says «Ella [Doña Margarita] a sus pies me verá / llorando hasta que consiga / vencer su severidad.» Doña Margarita is truely moved:

> Temí, recelé
> dar a tu amor incentivo,
> y sólo por correctivo
> severidad te mostré;
> mas oyéndote gemir
> cada noche desde el lecho,
> y a veces en tu despecho
> mis rigores maldecir,
> yo al Señor, de silencioso
> materno llanto hecha un mar,
> ofrecí mil veces dar
> mi vida por tu reposo.

ISABEL:

> Madre, ...
> mi aliento aquí exhalaré
> si no cedéis a mi lloro. *(Póstrase.)*

107

MARG.:

> Levanta, Isabel; enjuga
> tus ojos; confía. Sí:
> cuanto dependa de mí ...
> No, no, Isabel; cesa, cesa:
> yo en tu defensa me empeño;
> no será Azagra tu dueño   (act II, scene vi).

As mentioned before, what is much more characteristic of Romantic drama is not sentimentalism, but sensuality: the growth of emotionalism to the subsequent passion and extremes of melodrama and mysterious incidents. Scenes of recognition are constant.[6]

While scenes of recognition in the *comedia lacrimosa* were used for and had social implication, recognition remains part of the tradition of Romantic drama because of the feelings developed by surprise.

Alfredo is an excellent example of a Romantic drama which will reduce the lacrimose element somewhat, while developing the declamatory language and passionate or frenetic gestures. Act II, in keeping with the Romantic tradition of giving titles to the various acts, is entitled «Pasión». Alfredo describes the passion with which he is overcome to his friend Rugero: «¡Ay! tú no sabes el combate atroz que me desgarra mi pecho: tú ignoras los furores de la pasion que me consume.—No es una pasion humana ... es un amor frenético, infernal: es una llama irresistible; es un ascua de hierro candente, enterrada dentro del corazón ... En vano la he combatido, Rugero» (scene iv). In scene vii Alfredo, delirious, kills Jorge. In the final act Ricardo confronts his son with his horrible crimes. In the midst of thunder and lightening, Alfredo begs his father to take a sword and kill him. Since his father refuses Alfredo commits suicide. (*Al herirse Alfredo, aparece el Griego en el fondo. Véase en sus lábios una sonrisa infernal, y se desvanece. Horror general.*)

In *Don Álvaro o La fuerza del sino* we find an atmosphere of immense passion, mystery, murders, and suicides taking place against backgrounds in *chiaroscuro* or tempestuous storms.

El trovador offers three characters who are guided in their conduct only by their feelings and passions.

Azucena's speech in act III, scene i is an excellent example. She is still trembling with the horror of the memory she has revived of her mother. As in a trance, not realizing what she is saying, she continues her narrative to Manrique, describing her attempt at revenge and her frenzied error when she destroyed her own child instead of her enemy's: «Esta lucha era superior a mis fuerzas, y bien pronto se apoderó de mí una convulsión violenta ...; yo oía confusamente los chillidos del niño y aquel grito que me decía: '¡Véngame!' ... Un furor desesperado se apoderó de mí, y desatentada y frenética, tendí las manos buscando una víctima; la encontré, la así con una fuerza convulsiva, y la precipité entre las llamas.»

---

[6] *La conjuración de Venecia, Alfredo, Don Álvaro, El trovador, El paje, Doña Mencía* and *Simón Bocanegra* all contain moving scenes of recognition.

Leonor's words in scene iv of the same act are another example:

> Mas no puedo en mi inquietud
> arrancar del corazón
> esta violenta pasión
> que es mayor que mi virtud.

The conclusion of the play is melodramatic in the extreme. Leonor has begged mercy for Manrique but the Count refuses. As a last resource she offers to marry the Count if her lover may go free. So great is Nuño's passion for Leonor that he agrees. While he is giving orders to one of the guards, Leonor swallows poison. Manrique is freed but Leonor sinks to the floor at Manrique's feet as the poison claims its victim.

El paje is another succession of crimes, outrages and afflictions. The play is one huge outcry of passion:

FERRANDO:

> ¡Son delirios de mi mente!
> ¡Es delirio esta agonía
> Que, cada vez más ardiente,
> Me consume noche y día   (act II, scene vi).

DOÑA BLANCA:

> ... ¡Haz que yo olvide
> Una pasion frenética, que eterna
> Mi corazon abrasa y le devora,
> Dios de inmensa piedad! Ni es culpa mia.
> Tú que me diste un corazon de fuego,
> Tú que me hiciste débil, ¿por qué impío
> Gozarte quieres en el llanto mio? (act II, scene viii).

Ferrando goes into a wild frenzy after Doña Blanca kisses him:

FERRANDO:

> No; que el labio tuyo
> Helado lo sentí sobre una hoguera,
> Mi frente es un volcan, mis venas arden
> En fuego abrasador, irresistible ...

BLANCA:

> ¡Ferrando! ¡qué delirio! ...

FERRANDO:

> Sí, delirio,
> Que el alma emponzoñada alimentaba,
> Y mi sér y mi vida devoraba   (act III, scene viii).

II.   THE «SUBLIME» CRIMINAL

«As humanitarian ideas penetrated more and more into literature, the bandit ... [became] ... a secret benefactor, a nobleman with a dark past who devoted himself to a noble ideal, employs bandits as unconscious instruments of justice, and dreams of perfecting the world by committing crimes ... [He becomes an] apostle of Good.» So writes Mario Praz.[7]

One of the more important ways that sentimental comedy anticipated Romantic drama was in the development of a hero who represented virtue and vice simultaneously. These «sublime criminals» or outlaws became heroes because they embodied the rights of the individual against social prejudices and injustices. This concept incorporates Rousseau's idea that the so-called criminal is not born but made by circumstances; that society and civilization corrupt man who is naturally good. These heroes are essentially virtuous, sensitive beings. They defy customs, laws and traditions in a move toward social, moral and political liberty. But they are alone in their endeavors, feeling heartlessly rejected and abandonned by God and their fellow men. They view themselves as victims of a hostile fate. Their past is envelopped with mystery, often conjectured to be exalted.

Torcuato, in *El delincuente honrado,* combines virtue and vice. He is a criminal with an unknown past; «Pues este delincuente, este hombre proscripto, desdichado, aborrecido de todos, y perseguido en todas partes ... Soy yo mismo,» says Torcuato to Laura. «Soy un monstruo que está envenenando tu corazón y llenándolo de amargura» (act I, scene v). «Incierto de los autores de mi vida, he andado siempre sin patria ni hogar propio? (act I, scene iii). «¿Y adónde iré á esconder mi vida desdichada? ... Sin patria, sin familia, prófugo y desconocido sobre la tierra, ¿dónde hallaré refugio contra la adversidad?» (scene vi).

Torcuato is a murderer, but his crime can be justified. Anselmo, his loyal friend defends him: «Es verdad que has muerto al marqués de Montilla; pero lo hiciste insultado, provocado y precisado á defender tu honor» (act I, scene iii). Torcuato, too, justifies his criminal act: «El honor, que fué la única causa de mi delito, es, Señor, la única disculpa que pudiera alegar; pero esta excepcion no la aprecian las leyes» (act IV, scene iii).

Torcuato's praiseworthy character is well established:

LAURA:

Sí, padre mio; él está inocente y es muy digno de vuestra proteccion. ¡Ah! en su alma virtuosa no caben el dolor y la perversidad que caracterizan los delitos   (act III, scene vii).

DON JUSTO:

La virtud y generosidad de don Torcuato excitan mi compasion
(act III, scene viii).

Tu virtud me encanta   (act IV, scene iii).

Another example of the virtuous and satanic combined in a single hero is found in the protagonist of *El precipitado.*[8] Cándida describes Don

---

[7] *The Romantic Agony* (New York: Meridian Books, 1956), p. 78.
[8] For a discussion of this as well as other Romantic elements in *El precipitado* see Russell P. Sebold's article «El incesto, el suicidio y el primer romanticismo español,» *Hispanic Review,* 41, No. 4 (Autumn, 1973), 669-692.

Amato as «el egemplar de los Jóvenes nobles; ... es el mancebo mas bien hecho, mas bien educado, mas generoso que tiene Sevilla ... ¡Que corazon! ... es la persona mas digna del pueblo» (act I, scene i).

His only real crime is that he loves. But his love for Cándida, his supposed sister, is incestuous and therefore forbidden by society. «Dexemos esta cruel habitacion,» he declares. «Busquémos la piedad en el fin del Universo: Cándida, i Amato en un desierto harán la sociedad mas afortunada. Vamos, esposa mia» (act III, scene iii). «El Cielo me prohibe el amarte ... io te amo» (act V, scene ii). Even the way he views his crime is dualistic: «Incestuoso! terrible idea! o virtud! o delito!» (act V, scene i). Don Prudencio, his father, underscores this dualism when he speaks of «la edad de la ternura, i del furor!» (act III, scene vi).

The hero of *El vinatero de Madrid* is a proud, virtuous man with a mysterious past. Angelita describes the moral excellence of her father:

> Qué buen padre el mio! En él
> existen con todo imperio
> la providad, el honor,
> y la virtud. Yo no veo
> cosa en su merced, que no
> sea admirable. Qué genio
> tiene tan dulce, y amable!
> Con que nobles sentimientos
> me ha criado en medio de
> la miseria en que nos vemos!
> Su corazon generoso...   (act I).

But Juan also has his satanic side. He killed a man, while defending his honor and is willing to risk killing another.

Rufino, in the *comedia lacrimosa* entitled *Rufino y Aniceta,* is the perfect example of a virtuous, prudent, gentle being who is corrupted by society. The prejudices and injustices of Aniceta's father lead him to criminal thoughts: «la satisfaccion sangrienta / y criminal que he resuelto / ... pero antes / mi ribal su sangre vierta» (act II). Having been denied the hand of the girl he loves because he is poor, he will challenge his rival. He curses his outcast state: «porque mi adversa / suerte lo ha querido así. / Infeliz de mí! ... (act II).

The hero of *Las vivanderas ilustres* is a kind, generous, honorable soldier but he is also a transgressor. Jacinto killed one man while defending his honor and now plans to take the life of the Colonel. From a more humane standpoint, he would be considered innocent since he is simply defending his honor and that of his sweetheart Gertrudis, whom the Colonel has badly abused and bullied:

> No me consterna este estado
> tan desgraciado y funesto;
> no haberle dado la muerte
> solamente es lo que siento,
> porque así satisfacia
> el insulto que me ha hecho   (act I).

Gertrudis begs mercy for Jacinto. She goes before the Marquis to proclaim his innocence and declare that he is only the victim of his powerful enemy:

> Que su inocencia
> le lleva al suplicio. Que
> su muerte no será pena,
> sino victima inmolada
> á la crueldad mas sangrienta
> de un poderoso enemigo.

MARQ.:

> Sabes su culpa?

GERT.:

> Su culpa,
> no Señor: su suerte adversa,
> su virtud y honor si sé: (act II).

The heroine of *Natalia y Carolina* views herself as a pariah. She has been rejected and abandonned by all those whom she loved:

> un amor incomparable
> me roba el amor paterno
> ... ...
> ¿Contra una infeliz muger
> pueden combinarse á un tiempo
> mas desgracias? Carolina
> me amenaza con sus zelos:
> Aleman huye mis ansias
> á pesar de mis desvelos:
> y mi padre...
> ...viene á buscarme
> para desfogar su ceño.
> ... ...
> Todo, todo me amenaza:
> mi Padre, mis sentimientos,
> Carolina...   (act I).

Jacinto, in *El amor perseguido y la virtud triunfante,* is another example of a being who feels bitter about the contrast between his treatment by society and his own worth. He feels resentful that his noble character, his pure and sensitive soul, should be heartlessly rejected by his fellow-man:

> ...aborrezco
> estos momentos infaustos
> de vida que gozo, y solo
> mi pena, y continuo llanto
> son en esta soledad,
> los compañeros mas gratos
> á mi mal   (act II).

This virtuous, sensitive man is condemned to live a life of loneliness and despair.

Another example of this new hero-anti-hero of the tearful comedy is found in *Las víctimas del amor, Ana y Sindhám*. Both Ana and Sindhám are decent, praiseworthy beings. Ana has secretly married Sindhám against her father's will. In her quest for social and moral liberty, she was willing to defy her father and existing conventions. Her father's attitudes demonstrate the type of injustice against which she rebels:

> MILORD:
>
> Yo no tengo
> dominio sobre su gusto;
> como padre, le poseo
> sobre su persona   (act I).

Like the typical Romantic rebel, she is alone in her endeavor, rejected by all who surround her:

> En fin, Sindhám,
> Ya los cielos han querido
> que pierda por ti mi patria,
> mi casa, y el amor mismo
> de mi padre   (act II).

She is the victim of a hostile fate: «Ana infeliz, en qué dia / tan horrible y tan funesto / naciste! » (act I).

The treatment of the outlaw found in the *comedia lacrimosa* was generally contained by the narrow use to which it was put. The strict and unyielding nature of laws and conventions were under scrutiny, and developing empathy for their victims was the way in which the playwright further supported his social critique. The uses to which the outlaw is put in Romantic literature are different and respond to the Romantic artist's developing egocentrism. As Romantic drama evolves, the pariah soon becomes the most compelling of characters. First because, in the Rousseauistic sense, he represents the innocence of impulse against the strictures of convention, later merely because of the fascinating personality of the rebel, and finally because of aesthetics.

Again, what has happened is, in the *comedia lacrimosa,* the convention of the outlaw is used to support ideas. Later, in Romantic drama, in the larger Romantic tradition, and finally in the latest stages of Romantic development known as decadence, this figure of the pariah is used simply to stir emotion. As the purpose shifts, the nature of the outlaw shifts from that of a conventional character caught up in some violation of specific laws and customs, to one who is generally in opposition to society, to one whose character becomes constantly more satanic, and finally to one whose physical beauty matches the violence and desperation of his act.[9]

The protagonist of *La conjuración de Venecia* is a «noble savage.» He was raised and educated among humble people and later captured by

---

[9] The tradition culminates in the homoerotic novels of Jean Genet.

8

pirates. His virtues are described by various characters in the play. Laura speaks of Rugiero's sensitive soul: «es pobre, desvalido; ¡pero tiene un alma tan noble! ... ¡Es tan honrado, tan compasivo, tiene un corazón tan hermoso!» (act III, scene ii). The ambassador speaks of his loyalty and patriotism: «ama mucho a su patria adoptiva, y no piensa sino en salvarla» (act I, scene ii). Finally Rossi notes: «es tan bondadoso» (act V, scene ii). But, according to the values of the conservative society in which he lives, he is guilty of a criminal act. He conspired against the existing government. His actions would be considered heroic from a more liberal viewpoint since he was searching for political freedom against a tyrannical regime which denied citizens their rights. He was fighting against «la forma de gobierno de aquella república [Venice in the beginnings of the fourteenth century], la severidad de sus leyes, el rigor y el misterio de algunos de sus tribunales ...» (Martínez de la Rosa's *Advertencia* to this play).

Rugiero is a rebel who is willing to sacrifice his life for a noble ideal: «¡Venecia y libertad!» He is a typical Romantic hero, alone, rejected («yo soy ese objeto miserable de la ira del cielo y de los hombres» [act II, scene v]), abandonned, unhappy, with a mysterious past: «Yo, infeliz de mí, desque que abrí los ojos, no he tenido en el mundo a quien volverlos! ... Solo, huérfano, sin amparo ni abrigo ..., sin saber a quiénes debo el ser, ni siquiera la tierra en que nací ... ¿Por qué me amas, Laura, por qué me amas? Basta que seas mía, para que seas desgraciada» (act II, scene iii). Rugiero is a messianic figure, a savior or redeemer. The play abounds in biblical and religious allusions, typical of Romantic works, and also prevalent in the *comedia lacrimosa.*

The protagonist of *Alfredo* also represents virtue and vice combined in a single portagonist. Ángela speaks of Alfredo's «bello corazon» (act II, scene ii). Rugero, his dear friend, describes Alfredo as a baron deserving of the greatest estem: «Alfredo se distinguia entre todos los barones de Sicilia por la rectitud de su corazon y por la modestia de sus acciones; ... la única pasion que conmovia su pecho era el amor filial» (act IV, scene i). Alfredo also has his satanic side. He is a murderer, having killed Berta's brother. He is a rebel in the grand manner, willing to defy all social conventions and laws to satisfy his lust and pleasure. When speaking of his incestuous love and passion for his stepmother he declares: «Yo prefiero estos horrores, á esa inocencia vana é insípida de que me hablabas» (act III, scene vii).

Alfredo experiences Romantic solitude, rejection and abandonment: «¡No me entiende! ... ¡Nadie me entiende! ... » (act I, scene ii). «¡Todos me abandonan! ¡todos se separan de mi lado con horror ... ¿Llevaré por ventura como Cain la marca de la maldicion divina? ...» (act III, scene x). «¡Padre! ... ¡padre mio! ... ¿por qué me abandonais ahora que va á principiar mi arrepentimiento?» (act V, scene vii). He speaks of an adverse fate of which he is a victim: «¡La fatalidad! ... ¿No seremos todos sino débiles instrumentos de su poder; vanos juguetes de sus arcanos misteriosos? ... Entonces ... no había remedio; yo seré arrastrado, como la rama que cayó en el torrente» (act II, scene iv).

114

The diabolic and satanic are suggested constantly in the final act of *Don Álvaro o La fuerza del sino.* Don Álvaro is also virtuous and satanic. He is a devil from the conservative point of view. But his crimes can be justified. He is a murderer, having killed El Marqués de Calatrava, Don Carlos de Vargas and Don Alfonso de Vargas. In the first case, the Marquis' death was an accident, Álvaro's pistol going off as he threw it to the ground to remain unarmed. In the other two cases the men died as the result of a duel to which Don Álvaro was challenged, and which he only finally accepted to defend his wounded honor.

This play, like many sentimental comedies, contains commentaries against the rigid laws which do not distinguish between the provoked and the provoker in duels: «Lo cierto es que la ley es dura; pena de muerte por batirse; pena de muerte por ser padrino; pena de muerte por llevar cartas» (act IV, scene ii). «Pero ¡que pena tan dura, / tan extraña, tan violenta! ... / ¡La ley es atroz, horrenda! » (scene vi).

We know that Don Álvaro is essentially a noble, virtuous being. Preciosilla speaks of his generosity. We know of his benevolence, heroism and love for his fellow man through his actions towards Don Carlos in Italy. He is another example of Rousseau's «noble savage,» having been schooled among the beauties of nature away from the corruption of society: «Que una cárcel fué mi cuna, / Y fué mi escuela el desierto, / Entre bárbaros crecí» (act III, scene iii). Don Alfonso confirms Álvaro's declarations: «Tu entre los indios creciste, / Como fiera te educaste» (act V, scene ix).

In spite of his sensitive soul and noble character, he is a victim of the prejudices of the conservative European aristocracy. He is viewed as an outcast because of his obscure origin and mixed blood. He feels that a cruel, adverse Fate is always working against him, and speaks of «mi adversa estrella» (act I, scene vii).

> ¡Qué carga tan insufrible
> Es el ambiente vital,
> Para el mezquino mortal
> Que nace en signo terrible!   (act III, scene iii).

Even though his origin is unknown, he instinctively feels his nobility and has great pride: «Protector de mi estirpe soberana» (act I, scene vii).

The same type of dualism is evident in Don Manrique, in García Gutiérrez' *El trovador.* The loving way he treats Azucena is indicative of his upright nature: «Que me importa un nombre?» Manrique asks. «Mi corazón es tan grande como el de un rey! » (act III, scene i). His sin is his abduction of a nun from her cell in a convent. He has been denied the woman he loves because of his unknown and supposedly non illustrious background. He is willing to fight for his social and moral rights. Leonor expresses their dilemma: « ¡Ay juventud malograda, / por tiranos perseguida! » (act V, scene vii). Manrique and Leonor curse their «negra fortuna»:

> LEONOR:
>
> Llorando, sí;
> Yo para llorar nací;

mi negra estrella enemiga,
mi suerte lo quiere así.
Despreciada, aborrecida
del que amante idolatré
¿Qué es ya para mí la vida?   (act I, scene iii).

When Marsilla, the hero of *Los amantes de Teruel,* finally returns to his home and discovers that his lover Isabel is married to Don Rodrigo de Azagra, he becomes rebellious and finds himself envelopped with criminal thoughts. The following scene with his father is a good example of his struggle to regain the woman he loves at any cost.

MART.:
Hijo, modera ese furor.

MARS.:
La desventura quiebra
los vínculos del hombre con el hombre
y con la vida y la virtud. Ahora,
que tiemble mi rival, tiemble la mora.
Breve será su victorioso alarde:
para acabar con ambos, aún no es tarde.

MART.:
¡Desgraciado! ¿Qué intentas?

MARS.:
Con el crimen
el crimen castigar. Una serpiente
se me enreda en los pies; mi pie destroce
su garganta infernal. Un enemigo
me aparta de Isabel: huya o perezca.

MART.:
Hijo . . .

MARS.:
Perecerá
… … … … … … … … … … … … … …

MART.:
Merézcate respeto
ese lazo . . .

MARS.:
Es sacrílego, es injusto.

MART.:
En presencia de Dios formado ha sido.

MARS.:
Con mi presencia queda destruído   (act III, scene xi).

Don Martín represents the conservative viewpoint. What the laws and customs of society dictate are right, and therefore, must be respected. Marsilla stands for the «new order.» In order for laws and conventions to be upheld, they must be concerned, above all, with the individual and his feelings. Laws which lack this concern are made to be broken.

García Gutiérrez wrote two plays with revolutionaries as their heroes. Simón Bocanegra, the hero of the play with a title bearing his name, is virtuous in every way: generous, brave, prudent and upright. He is a pirate who has been elevated from his humble station to Doge of Genova because of his dignified and noble character. Like Rugiero, in *La conjuración de Venecia,* he is willing to lead an uprising against the nobility in an effort to obtain political and social freedom: «romperé osado / Las infames cadenas que le [el pueblo] oprimen» (Prologue, scene v).

Juan Lorenzo, the Valencian wool-dresser of *Juan Lorenzo,* is also a simple man raised to the ranks of leader and concerned with obtaining political liberty for his fellow-men, who have been deprived of their natural rights: «Libertad tiene por nombre; / Aclamadla, y que del seno / De nuestras desdichas brote» (act II, scene vii). He views his role as that of a savior:

> ¡Grande es nuestra empresa: hacer
> Á tantos peligros frente,
> Y alcanzar la redencion
> Para un pueblo que padece,
> ... ...
> Que hombres somos, y no esclavos   (act II, scene xi).

It is appropriate to conclude this discussion of the Romantic rebel by examining the greatest anti-hero of all—Don Juan, in Zorrilla's play *Don Juan Tenorio.* Don Juan is related to Prometheus and Faust, but through the nature of his rebellion he is brought closer to us than are these two epic heroes. Don Juan rebels against the established order not through promotion of abstract theory but by an indulgence in the concrete sensual pleasures of this world at the possible expense of an unknown price in the next. For Don Juan is not so much a challenger of eternity; he is not interested in it. Rather than trying to disprove God or eternity, he is more concerned with the rhythm of existence, implying the greatest blasphemy of all—that is, that perhaps the joys of this world are great enough to compensate for the punishment of eternity. The character who can maintain such an idea is a formidable opponent to established order. It is this potency that makes him so compelling a figure.

Don Juan is a typical incarnation of Romanticism with his insistence on unchecked individual liberty.[10] He is the symbol of the rebellious or combative man against the forces around him that threaten to rob him of his spirit, his freedom, his will, his *yo.*

His satanic nature is constantly alluded to throughout the play. His

---

[10] Mérimée, Musset, Dumas, *père,* Byron, Baudelaire, Espronceda and Zorrilla all made Don Juan the hero of their nineteenth century works.

father calls him «el monstruo de liviandad» (act I, scene viii), and «hijo de Satanás» (scene xii); the sculptor, «un aborto del abismo,» (Part II, act I, scene ii) and «Lucifer.» Doña Inés cannot resist him: «Tal vez Satán puso en vos / su vista fascinadora, / su palabra seductora» (Part I, act IV, scene iii).

III. THE DRAMATIC INTERPRETATION OF *Fastidio Universal*

The physical emptiness and abandonment that these Romantics heroes experience is reflected in their milieu which is pictured as unjust, and lacking in either compassion or understanding. This union of the spiritual and the physical leads to the universalization of the Romantic's grief. Suicide, a theme dear not only to the Romantics, but also frequently found in lachrymose comedy, was often viewed as the only possible relief from their malaise, wearisomeness, *fastidio universal* or *Weltschmerz*. However, suicide is really only a device in the *comedia lacrimosa* to make the viewer empathize further with the character and the point of view he represents. In the Romantic tradition a preoccupation with suicide and death is merely a further move on a continuum of sensuality and eroticism. Death is one more idea which is used by the Romantic artist for the quality of feeling that the contemplation of it evokes.

Torcuato, in *El delincuente honrado,* expresses his disgust and grief: «El cielo me ha condenado á vivir en la adversidad. ¡Qué desdichado nací! » (act I, scene iii). Laura wishes to accompany her husband in death as in life: « ¡Qué! Despues de perderle, ¿me negarán tambien el consuelo de morir en sus brazos?» (act IV, scene viii). «Dejadme, dejadme que vaya á acompañarle; que la sangrienta espada corte á un mismo tiempo nuestros cuellos» (act V, scene v).

The protagonist of *El precipitado* expresses his grief in the same cosmic terms used by the Romantic hero: «Muramos, pues:: mi delito, i mi desventura estan en no olvidarla:: pongamos fin a mi delito:: muramos, i seamos felices::: no bolverla a ver, i ser felices! ... Detestado de toda la creacion, insepulto, i abominado, io sería el destructor de la obra del Altísimo, el obgeto de la exêcración universal, la fúnebre causa del perpetuo llanto de todos los mios::: la casa, la ciudad, el reino, todo el mundo sabría su desgracia: sabría la mia ... Mi espada sera el executor de mi decreto ... Ia resuelto, estoi con mas sosiego, i parece que comienzo a sentir el descanso de la nada a que voi a reducirme» (act V, scene i).

Notice how similar the words of Federica are in the sentimental comedy *Eduardo y Federica*: «La justicia eterna me condena á huir hasta de los buenos, y á pasar mis dias, solo entre las fieras ... Mis penas deben acompañarme hasta el sepulcro! ... Soy tan criminal! ... Soy tan digna de la execracion de los hombres! ... Mi existencia es tan amarga! ... Ay! cuan agradable me será la muerte! (act I).

Another example which shows the psychological tie between the individual and the universal is found in the Romantic drama *Alfredo* when Berta declares: «he sido el oprobio de mi país, el escándalo de Sicilia,

118

la execracion del mundo todo! ... ¡Enormes han sido mis crímenes! ...
Mi existencia ha sido un azote para la humanidad! ... (act V, scene iv).

Returning to the *comedia lacrimosa* for more examples of this *mal àu
siècle,* the words of Juan in *Cecilia la cieguecita* are reminiscent of those of
Tediato in Cadalso's *Noches lúgubres.* Both suffer at the mercy of «la risa
universal.»

> Ya ¿qué me queda? Morir,
> morir solo. ¿Qué me importa
> la vida, si es un tormento
> cada dia, cada hora;
> si entre pesares contínuos
> ha de ser triste, afanosa;
> si una mano en este mundo
> no encuentro consoladora
> que mis lágrimas enjugue,
> que me apoye en mis congojas;
> ... ...
> debiendo ser de las gentes
> desde hoy mas escarnio y mofa?
> Sí, sí, mas vale morir   (act III, scene ix).

Delio, in *El amor dichoso,* and Jacinto in *El amor perseguido y la
virtud triunfante,* long for the peaceful moments of life eternal as relief
from this wearisome, cruel, inhumane existence.

> DELIO:
>
> Tristes recuerdos!
> memorias desventuradas!
> huyamos de este funesto
> lugar para siempre: ...
> ...mísero destino!
> ella me dexa, Y yo á morir camino.
> ... Yo no espero
> sobrevivir á tu culpa:
> voy a exâlar mis postreros
> suspiros...   (act I).
>
> JACINTO:
>
> ...mi corazon amargo
> ...esta esperando
> con ansia, aquel dulce instante
> postrero, de este cansado
> aliento mio: aborrezco
> estos momentos infaustos
> de vida que gozo, y solo
> mi pena, y contínuo llanto
> son en esta soledad,
> los compañeros mas gratos
> a mi mal   (act II).

My final example, is taken from the lachrymose comedy *Las víctimas
del amor, Ana y Sindhám*:

119

SINDHÁM:

En diez años
no ví dia sin martirio,
noche sin desasosiego,
noche sin grande peligro,
ni instante sin sobresalto,
y por fin hoy, se han unido
todos á afligirme...
... Ah, Sindhám triste,
qué lexos está el alivio
de tus penas!...
Pues que medio, qué camino
seguirás, Sindhám, en tantas
angustias? Qual? El mas digno
de un corazon ya cansado
de lidiar con su destino:
el morir: sí, sí, muramos ` (act II).

Ana wants to die with Sindhám:

Yo aborrezco
esta exîstencia: mi vida
es ya de ningun provecho
en el mundo.
Ahora...
penas acabad mi vida
... ...
No, durmais, pesares;
venid, matadme aprisa;
Cielo inhumano!   (act III).

Returning to Romantic drama for more examples of this *Weltschmerz* and consequent suicide, or double suicide, Laura, in *La conjuración de Venecia,* describes the pitiless, unsympathetic world of Rugiero: «No merece el rigor con que le ha tratado la suerte ... El no tiene más esperanza en el mundo que las lágrimas de su esposa» (act III, scene ii). She will either save him or die at his side: «Yo nací para ti, Rugiero; para consolarte en tus penas, para hacerte olvidar tu orfandad y llenar el vacío de tu corazón» (act II, scene iii). «No lo temas, Rugiero, no lo temas; tu Laura te salvará o morirá contigo» (act III, scene i).

Death is the solution to the insufferable existence of Macías and Elvira in Larra's drama.

MACÍAS:

¿Qué es la vida?
Un tormento insufrible...
...buscando
voy mi muerte;
La vida arráncame...
¡Desventurado!   (act III, scene iv).

ELVIRA:

> que morirá si mueres...
> Primero que ser suya, entrambos juntos
> muramos.

MACÍAS:

> Sí, muramos

ELVIRA:

> ¡Los cielos me abandonan!   (act IV, scene iii).

Elvira takes her life when she discovers that Macías has been murdered by Fernán Pérez.

ELVIRA:

> *(Enseñando la daga a Fernán Pérez.)*
> La tumba será el ara donde pronta
> la muerte nos despose.
> *(Se hiere y cae al lado de Macías.)*
> Dichosa
> muero contigo   (act IV, scene iv).

Alfredo describes his grief in the same cosmic terms as Berta: «Yo soy el oprobio de vuestro nombre, el baldon de Sicilia, la execración del mundo... un golpe solo; y se borra ese oprobio... y Alfredo descenderá al eterno descanso! Mi muerte, mi muerte sola» *(Alfredo,* act V, scene vi). «¿Dónde... ¿dónde pudo encontrar, no ya la ventura, siquiera al menos el descanso? ... ¿dónde? ... ¡Ah! lo sé ... En un lugar ... en un lugar solo ... no hay más que uno para mí ... la tumba. ¡La tumba! sí ... y bajaré a ella ... yo descansaré en el seno de la nada ... Allí, allí se calmarán estos dolores: allí se apagará la maldecida estrella que me ha conducido por el mundo» (act V, scene i).

The same universalization of the Romantic's grief is found in *Don Álvaro, El trovador* and *El paje*:

DON ALVARO:

> Yo no soy mas que un réprobo, presa infeliz del demonio! Mis palabras sacrílegas aumentarían vuestra condenación. Estoy manchado de sangre, estoy irregular   (act. V, scene ix).
>
> ¡Terrible cosa es nacer!
> ... ...
> Y yo que infelice soy,
> Yo que buscándola [la muerte] voy,
> ... ¡Terrible suerte!
> Que en ella reina la muerte,
> Ya la muerte busco yo   (act III, scene iii).

LEONOR:

> Ya no hay en el universo
> nada que me haga apreciar
> esta vida que aborrezco.

Aqui, ...
no veré, amiga, a lo menos
a esos tiranos impíos
que causa de mi mal fueron.

... ...
Estoy resuelta, ya no hay
felicidad, ni la quiero,
en el mundo para mí;
sólo morir apetezco   (*El trovador,* act II, scene vi).

FERRANDO:
Busco la muerte.

... ...
Miradme; que en mi edad florida,
  (Bebiendo del pomo.)
Sin miedo alguno el tósigo derramo
En este corazon lleno de vida.
Ahora decidme si estaré resuelto,
Ya sin amor, sin esperanza alguna   (*El paje,* act. IV, scene ix).

One of the most important causes of the universalization of the Romantic's grief was «the sensorial projection of the poet's mood onto all the faces of the universe.»[11] There was a new marriage or rapport between man's soul and nature. Nature became a confidant, and being in accord with man's sentiments, reiterated his feelings. Even this notion of nature as an appendage of man's spirit was foreshadowed in the *comedia lacrimosa.*

Torcuato describes a ficticious ambience, which is simply an exteriorization of his internal feelings: «Laura, consuélate; yo voy á vengarte ... Voy á huir de tí para siempre, y á esconder mi vida detestable en los horribles climas donde no llega la luz del sol, y donde reinan siempre el horror y la obscuridad» *(El delincuente honrado,* act II, scene v).

In *El amor dichoso,* there is a perfect correspondence between Dantéo's mood and the scene which surrounds him. When Dantéo is happy, his milieu is viewed as beautiful and soothing:

Quán apacible y hermosa
la mañana está! Qué fresco
vientecillo corre! Y quánto
nos hace mas alhagüeño
y grato el sitio el susurro
blando que forma moviendo
continuamente las hojas
de esos arboles! Que bello
presentan ahora á la vista
este monte, los reflexos
que le presta el sol! Los campos,
de verde yerba cubiertos,
qual brillan con el rocío
del alba!   (act I).

[11] RUSSELL P. SEBOLD, «Enlightenment Philosophy and the Emergence of Spanish Romanticism,» p. 131.

dismal and gloomy when he is sad:

> ...el valle
> sombrio está, está funesto
> sin su vista: si esos campos
> que ostentaban otro tiempo
> su lozania, están mustios
> porque no la ven: y en fin,
> si ese blanco álamo bello
> que la arrulló tantas veces,
> con el blando y lisongero
> rumor de sus hojas, hoy
> parece que está suspenso   (act I).

Nature reiterates Berta's melancholy in the drama *Alfredo*: «Los cora-zones tristes se complacen en la soledad; y estas dulces y melancólicas no-ches de Sicilia» (act II, scene vi). She projects how lovely nature will be when she is happy: «El sol nacerá todos los dias brillante y magestuoso: la noche se levantará siempre suave y placentera: mi vida, mi vida toda, va á ser una contínua ilusion» (act III, scene vii). An excellent example of the projection of the personal upon the universal is found in the final act of this play. Ricardo, Alfredo's father, having returned to Sicily after his long absence, confronts the transgressions of his son and wife: «¡Ojalá la hu-biese yo acompañado á la tumba ... *(Abre una ventana del fondo; y aparece el Volcan ardiendo. Relámpagos y truenos.—Vuelve á cerrar.)* ¡Oh Dios! ¡también el cielo ... también la naturaleza se estremece! ... ¿Qué noche de horrores es esta! ¿qué noche de desolación!» (act V, scene iii). *(Truenos)* «¡Cómo brama la tempestad! Parece que batallan todos los elemen-tos ... que el universo entero se conmueve como mi corazon!» (scene v).

Manrique's description of the peaceful night he met Leonor is simply a reflection of the bliss he felt:

> En una noche plácida y tranquila...
> ¡qué recuerdo, Leonor; ...
> ...la luna hería
> con moribunda luz tu frente hermosa,
> y de la noche el aura silenciosa
> nuestros suspiros tiernos confundía
>
> *(El trovador,* act III, scene v).

How different the night is for Ferrando from the placid, tranquil one described by Manrique:

> Mas oscura
> Que el hondo porvenir, negra, horrora
> Cual la noche fatal que me arrancara
>
> *(El paje,* act II, scene vii).

A final example is found in *Don Juan Tenorio*. Don Juan's happiness is reflected in a nature characterized by peace, harmony, and tranquility:

¡Ah! ¿No es cierto, ángel de amor,
que en esta apartada orilla
más pura la luna brilla
y se respira mejor?
Esta aura que vaga, llena
de los sencillos olores
de las campesinas flores
que brota esa orilla amena;
esa agua limpia y serena
... ...
¿no es cierto, paloma mía,
que están respirando amor?
Esa armonia que el viento
recoge entre esos millares
de floridos olivares,
que agita con manso aliento;
ese dulcísimo acento
con que trina el ruiseñor

(Part I, act IV, scene iii).

IV. THE LUGUBRIOUS AND TENEBRIFIC

There are lugubrious, gloomy elements in both the *comedia lacrimosa* and Romantic drama which accentuate the sentimental, sullen, dismal and wearisome mood of these plays. These elements may be found in the vocabulary, music, and the ambience of the play, which often consists of night scenes in *chiaroscoro* in towers or dungeons, often with the accompaniment of a tempestuous storm.

Let us compare the sets in *El delincuente honrado* and *La conjuración de Venecia*, when both protagonists await their execution.

Act IV of Jovellanos' play is set in a dismal tower. «*El teatro representa el interior de una torre del alcázar, que sirve de prision á Torcuato. La escena es de noche. En esta habitacion no habrá mas adorno que dos ó tres sillas, una mesa, y sobre ella una bujía.*» [12] In act V, as Torcuato is in prison, with chains, awaiting his execution, we hear the incessant tolling of the dismal bell and the somber military music: «*sonará á lo léjos música militar lúgubre,*» and «*la fúnebre campana*» (scene iii). In the final act phrases such as the following are used: *la lúgubre vestidura, el funesto pregón de la sentencia, la hora funesta, un abismo de afliccion y miseria, este melancólico silencio.*

In act II of *La conjuración de Venecia* «*el teatro representa el panteón de la familia Morosini: vense a entrambos lados varios sepulcros, con estatuas y emblemas fúnebres ... y alumbra con una lámpara.*» Three times the rustling of the wind is mentioned. This gloomy set in *chiaroscuro* is the background for Rugiero's telling Laura of his plans to overthrow the

---

[12] Compare the set of act IV of *Macías:* «*Prisión de Macías. Puerta a la izquierda y derecha; ...Una lámpara encendida.*»

government. In the final act, the *mise en scène* is a courtroom for Rugiero's trial. Rugiero is being held in the torture chamber. «*El teatro representa la sala de audiencia del Tribunal de los Diez, de aspecto opaco y lúgubre; en el promedio formará una especie de media luna ... Es de noche, una lámpara antigua alumbra escasamente la estancia.*» The bells toll incessantly, as they did in *El delincuente honrado*, as Rugiero awaits his execution. The vocabulary is no less dreary: *un máscara vestido de negro, un presentimiento fatal, sepulcro, la noche tan oscura, mal agüero, panteón tan triste.*

Act V, scene i of *El precipitado* is a night scene in *chiaroscuro. Don Amato solo. Con todas las señales de la mas negra desesperacion: trae en una mano una bugía encendida.* The set accentuates Amato's despair when he discovers his love is incestuous and therefore forbidden, and his plans for suicide. Words such as *espectro, fantasma, rebelde, execración universal, funesto, negra, desesperación* are utilized throughout the play.

Wilson's plans for suicide, in *El fabricante de paños,* are accompanied by gloomy, dismal sets. In the first instance the *chiaroscuro* of a poorly lit room: «*El teatro estará obscuro por ser la scena de noche. Sale Vilson por la izquierda trayendo una luz que pondrá sobre la mesa, caminando con la mas profunda tristeza*» (act III); in the second, the *chiaroscuro* of the moonlit square in front of Westminster Bridge in act IV. Wilson, *confundido de dolor,* or *anegado en su dolor,* speaks of his *fatal desdicha,* his *sepulcro,* and his *negra suerte.*

In act III of *Las vivanderas ilustres,* the misery of Gertrudis, as her lover is about to be executed, is underscored by the tenebrous set and the gloomy music in the background: «*Gertrudis que vestirá luto ... tocan la marcha ... teniendo el teatro poca luz* (pues ya la noche / sus lobregueces dilata).»

Aben Humeya offers an excellent example of a play whose sets complement the action. As the conspirators are making their plans, «*el teatro se va oscureciendo.*» They meet in a cave and «*una lámpara de hierro alumbra escasamente ese especie de gruta, mientras lo restante del teatro aparece sombrio*» (act I, scene vii). During the hostilities, when the Moors set fire to the Christian's church, «*óyese el toque de una campana, los ecos del órgano, y el eco de las aclamaciones de los instrumentos militares. El incendio de la iglesia va en aumento; empiezan a caer puertas y ventanas, y dejan ver el interior del templo ardiendo, al mismo tiempo que está nevando a copos*» (act II, scene xiii).

The lugubrious and gloomy are suggested throughout *Alfredo* in the language—*oprobio, execración, el corazón me palpita, sumergido en alguna prisión horrorosa, tristeza dura y silenciosa, la espantosa aparición, una bendición sacrílega, este abismo sin fondo*—and in the sets. As the theme of incest is suggested for the first time, it is starting to get dark, and the action is set «*en el fondo del Etna.*» In act II, scene iv, Alfredo tells his friend of his passionate love for his stepmother. (*Durante esta escena ha anochecido completamente, y salido la luna.*) Act V, entitled «Crimen,» occurs in the castle of Alfredo. It is night. Ricardo, Alfredo's father, has returned to Sicily and learns of his son's incestuous affair with his wife. (*Abre una ventana del fondo; y aparece el Volcan ardiendo. Relámpagos y truenos.*)

—scene iii. As Berta admits her crime and Alfredo plans his suicide there are *(truenos hasta la conclusion.)*

Don Álvaro o La fuerza del sino has a similar conclusion. As a background for Álvaro's killing of Alfonso, Alfonso's killing of his sister Leonor and Don Álvaro's suicide, *«el teatro representa un valle rodeado de riscos inaccesibles*[13] *... Sobre un peñasco ... habrá una medio gruta, medio ermita con puerta practicable, y una campana que pueda sonar y tocarse desde dentro: el cielo representará el ponerse el sol de un día borrascoso, se irá obscureciendo lentamente la escena y aumentándose los truenos y relámpagos ... hay un rato de silencio: los truenos resuenan más fuertes que nunca, crecen los relámpagos, y se oye cantar a lo lejos el Miserere»* (act V, scene ix). In the previous acts there are night scenes in *chiaroscuro,* set in a forest,[14] cloister, cave and mounntain *(en la ladera de una áspera montaña. Al frente un profundo valle).*

The sets and vocabulary in *El trovador* are no less tenebrous and dreary. The action takes place in a tower, a cell, a dungeon and a gypsy cave lit by a bonfire, accompanied by a «lúgubre gemido,» or a «lúgubre clamor.» Words and phrases such as *mi negra estrella, la oscuridad profunda, la luna moribunda, mi pasion criminal, sombra, abismo, algún gemido melancólico, triste y lúgubre, el resplandor siniestro* are employed. In act V, Manrique is imprisoned in a dark dungeon. He is longing for death. While he hears a «lúgubre gemido,» *(se ve brillar un momento el resplandor de una luz en la ventana de la izquierda.)*

Marsilla tells of the frightening surroundings in which he found himself, in the first act of *Los amantes de Teruel:*

> Ayer, hoy mismo, ¿cuál era
> mi suerte? Sumido en honda
> cárcel, estrecha y hedionda,
> sin luz, sin aire siquiera,
> envuelto en infecta nube
> que húmedo engendra el terreno,
> paja corrompida, cieno
> y piedras por cama tuve   (scene iv).

A final example is found in the Romantic drama *Simón Bocanegra.* The entire prologue is a night scene in *chiaroscuro.* *«Una gran plaza de Génova. En el fondo, la iglesia de San Lorenzo, que se iluminará luego interiormente. A la derecha, el palacio de los Fiescos ... con un farolillo delante, que alumbrará esta parte de la escena.»* In scene xi of the Prologue, Simón is in the palace of the Fiescos looking for his sweetheart Mariana Fiesco who has not seen the light of day for three years.

---

[13] The *mise en scène* is similar in act III of *Las víctimas del amor, Ana y Sindhám,* where Sindhám plans his death: *«El teatro será un monte de alguna eminencia. Se va obscureciendo el Teatro.»*
[14] A dark, thick forest is the background for Federica's misery in the sentimental comedy *Eduardo y Federica.*

Boc.:

> ¡Todo es silencio y tinieblas!
> ¡Pavor y misterio todo!
> ... ...
> Aqui hay una luz... veamos.

(Descuelga el farol que alumbra á la Madona, y procura alumbrar con él en el interior del palacio; pero sin entrar.)

> ¡Allí... vive Dios! dudosos
> Negros fantasmas se pintan
> Sobre los muros, diabólicos.

Simón discovers that Mariana is dead.

V. Eroticism and Exoticism

Another consequence of this *mal du siècle* was a desire of evasion from this life; a freeing from reality by means of the imagination. A common Romantic element was a re-evocation of the voluptuous, exotic ambience of the Orient with all its corruption and richness. Orientalism is characterized by a mixture of the erotic and the exotic. In the Romantic inversion of values to which I referred earlier, vice represents the positive element, virtue the negative one. Eroticism in general, and incest in particular, was a theme dear to the Romantics. While Spanish Romantic literature contains examples of concupiscent behavior, it never reaches the levels of eroticism that characterized French literature of the same epoch in writers such as the Marquis de Sade, Chateaubriand and Baudelaire. Here too, the *comedia lacrimosa* announced what was to become prevalent in Romantic drama. I will compare *El precipitado* with *Alfredo,* two plays dealing with incest.

Don Amato longs for the voluptuousness of the Orient: «¿Por qué no nací io en los paises del Oriente donde no es delito amar a sus hermanas los tiernos hermanos?» (act V, scene i). This comment occurs in a play where the relatives of Amato undergo a series of captivities and other incidents in Tetuan, Cairo and Izmir. The exotic ambience of the Orient is accentuated by Don Justo's discussion of the riches brought from these foreign lands, and by details such as Justo's smoking a Turkish pipe or discussing the daily customs of the Dervish Ofman Agà: «repetia cada dia tres millones i medio de veces el nombre Alah: tenia mui larga la barba: se labava cinquenta veces al dia; gritava mucho en la torre de la Mosschit, i jamas bebia vino en la plaza» (act IV, scene viii).

In *Alfredo,* we not only find the incestuous, but also the satanic and hedonistic, expressed with all the Romantic ardor. The Greek, who is described as a type of devil («mofador eterno de todos los sentimientos generosos, despreciador de todas las cosas divinas, frio predicador de un ateísmo desolante» act IV, scene i), expresses this philosophy best: «Creedme: no hay nada de real y de positivo sino el placer ... Todo lo demás son quimeras y preocupaciones» (act III, scene vi).

Alfredo describes the frenetic and passionate love he feels for his step-mother Berta: «No es una pasion humana ... es un amor frenético, infernal: es una llama irresistible» (act II, scene iv). The satanic and hedonistic are emphasized in his declaration of love to Berta: «Yo os adoro: ... yo llevo el infierno mismo, el infierno del amor, dentro de mis entrañas ... ¡Maldicion, maldicion al que quiera impedirlo! ... Seamos felices un momento sólo, y despues ... que el infierno nos confunda. ¿Qué importa? Un instante; y venga, venga despues el rayo que nos aniquile! ...» (act II, scene vi). Now that their lives are dominated by evil, Alfredo recommends enjoying their pleasures to the utmost: «Nuestro destino ha sido horroroso; pero es necesario que se cumpla ... Nuestra vida está dominada por el mal ... enhorabuena. Le sufriremos; mas no dejaremos de amarnos ... no nos arrepentiremos de nuestra pasion ... Yo prefiero estos horrores, á esa inocencia vana é insípida» (act III, scene vii). Berta agrees: «Mi vida va á ser ... un sueño inacabable de placeres» (act III, scene vii).

Again in this play the theme of incest is combined with the exoticism of the Orient: Alfredo «irá á pedir al Oriente su felicidad ó su desgracia» (act I, scene i). «Partiré,» he says. «Por lo menos, un mundo que no conozco va á aparecer á mi presencia: una vida que no he experimentado va á ser en adelante mi vida» (scene ii).

The basis of *El paje* is Ferrando's love for Doña Blanca, who turns out to be his mother. His is a rapturous passion, an all-consuming love. The theme of incest and satanism are constantly suggested: «no sabe / Que es su madre la que ama?» asks Don Rodrigo (act IV, scene iv). Blanca's sister says to Ferrando: «¡Ay pajecillo! hasta hereje / Os va volviendo ese amor» (act II, scene v). After Doña Blanca declares her love for Ferrando, the latter exclaims: «Perdóname tú, Señor; / Que el ángel malo ha vencido» (act III, scene viii). Ferrando tells Blanca to be hedonistic: «vive para el placer» (act IV, scene ix). The only code Don Rodrigo is willing to obey is his own feelings and passion: «Si para ello debo cometer un crímen, le cometeré ... Un crímen que hará mi dicha: detras de él está la felicidad ó la muerte; pues bien, yo quiero lo uno ó lo otro» (act II, scene iii).

The theme of incest is also fundamental in *Doña Mencía* and *Alfonso el Casto*. In the former play, Doña Mencía has fallen in love with Don Gonzalo:

> Y decirme necesito
> mil veces á cada instante,
> que ese nombre que repito
> es de padre, y no de amante,
> y que es mi pasion delito   (act III, scene v).

The fact that her love turns out to be incestuous does not cause her to renounce their relationship:

> Yo te adoro;
> que en tí un amor inestinguible puse.
> ... ...
> El infierno á mi amor ha presidido.
> A mi padre encuentro en mi marido   (act III, scene xii).

Alfonso el Casto is the story of Alfonso's incestuous love for his sister Jimena. Bernarda, Alfonso's wet nurse, tricks Alfonso into declaring the «loca pasion» that he feels for Jimena. «Rey,» says Bernarda, «la tuya era un incesto» (act III, scene viii).

VI. A New Stylistic Medium: Prose

The *comedia lacrimosa* also foreshadowed Romantic drama in technical areas. The innovative use of prose in sentimental comedy paved the way for Spanish Romantic drama which, if not written entirely in prose, alternated prose with verse.

Martínez de la Rosa's two plays *Aben Humeya* and *La conjuración de Venecia* are written entirely in prose, as is Pacheco's *Alfredo*. In the *Advertencia* to *La conjuración de Venecia*, Martínez de la Rosa wrote a justification of his use of prose: «me propuse dar a los sentimientos, al estilo y al lenguaje la mayor naturalidad,» words that recall the *Advertencia del Impresor* preceeding *El precipitado* (1773-1774): Trigueros chose to write in prose because «le parece que la naturalidad, que huie del verso, i de la compresion, habita en la prosa.» Hartzenbusch also wrote two plays in prose entitled *La archiduquesita* and *La coja y el encojido*.

In most of the plays where there is an alternation of prose and verse, the scenes of local color and narration are often in prose. Such is the case in *Don Álvaro o La fuerza del sino, El trovador,* and *El paje*. In *El trovador* the servants speak in prose among themselves and with their masters; Manrique and Azucena, being of a lower social class, also speak in prose; but the upper classes (including Manrique and Leonor) speak in verse, which has traditionally been associated with the noble and the heroic. I could find no pattern for the use of verse and prose in *Los amantes de Teruel*.

VII. The Exclamatory Style

The exclamatory style, associated with deep emotional expression, and found in the *comedia lacrimosa,* is even more characteristic of Romantic drama. The Romantic plays increase the interrogations, apostrophes, abrupt interruptions, exclamations and leaders that were so evident in sentimental comedy.

Don Amato's soliloquy, which opens act V of *El precipitado,* is an excellent example of this exclamatory style. Since many excerpts from this long monologue have already been given, I will not repeat them here.

In *El Vinatero de Madrid,* the Marquis reflects upon his abandonment of Angelita:

> Es cierto,
> Don Nicasio: mas mi amor: : :
> su virtud: : : mis juramentos: : :
> aquella inocencia: : aquella
> hermosura: :   (act I).

129

Dantéo, fearing Belisa's abandonment in *El amor dichoso,* exclaims:

... Tristes recuerdos!
memorias desventuradas!
mal cumplidos juramentos!
Belisa me olvida: ay ansias!
Belisa me dexa: ay Cielos!   (act I).

Gertrudis shouts the following words as she hears several shots and believes her husband has been executed:

Mas mi esposo::: Mi Jacinto
Justo Dios! Mi vida acaba!
(*Las vivanderas ilustres,* act III).

As Federica contemplates suicide in act I of *Eduardo y Federica,* she cries out: «mi existencia es tan amarga! ... No señor, debo conservarla hasta que prueve el dolor de ver publicar mi culpa::: Entónces, ay! cuan agradable me será la muerte!»

A final example, found in sentimental comedy, comes from the second act of *Las víctimas del amor, Ana y Sindhám,* where Sindhám gives vent to his anguish:

Ay hija!
Ay Ana bella! Ah destino!
Ay triste Sindhám! Oh Cielos,
doleos de mi martirio!

Although Romantic drama abounds in examples, I will only give three. The first is taken from the play *Macías:*

MACÍAS:
¡Oh! ¡Lloren mis ojos! ¡Lloren noche y día!
... ...
¡Ay de quien al mundo para amar nació!
¡Ay de aquel que muere por una mujer ingrata!
(act IV, scene ii).

The second comes from *Alfredo:* «No, Berta ... No partireis ... no partiremos ... Imposible! ¡imposible! ... ¡Perezca mi virtud! ¡perezca todo! ... No puedo abandonaros ... La deshonra ... el crimen ... ¿qué me importa? No, no os abandonaré ... He luchado ... he resistido ... he querido huir ... imposible! ...» (act II, scene vi).

A final example, from *Don Álvaro o La fuerza del sino,* must have been the type of speech that inspired Mesonero Romanos to write his Romantic parody ¡¡Ella ... !!! y ¡¡El!!!, in his article «El romanticismo y los romanticos» (1837). Don Álvaro is recalling his beloved Andalucía while he is serving as a soldier in Italy:

¡Sevilla! ! ! ¡Guadalquivir! ! !
¡Cuál atormentáis mi mente! ...
Noche en que vi de repente
Mis breves dichas huir!
¡Oh qué carga es el vivir! ...
¡Cielos, saciad el furor!   (act III, scene iii).

VIII.   STAGE AND LOCAL COLOR

The scenes of local color and the detailed stage directions that characterized Romantic drama had their roots in sentimental comedy. The
lachrymose comedies were the first plays in the history of Spanish theater
which utilized detailed stage sets. The *comedia lacrimosa* was the product
of an age which placed great emphasis on accurate, detailed description
and on the sensations Nature impressed on the mind. In view of the fact
that examples of these elaborate sets have already been given in previous
chapters,[15] I will only give three models here.

The *mise en scène* of Valladares' *Rufino y Aniceta*:

ACTO PRIMERO

La escena se representa en la huerta de Cosme, que esta en un pueblo
inmediato á la Corte.

*Levantado el telon se descubrirá una huerta dilatada y deliciosa, con varios
árboles repartidos con órden, y uno muy grueso á cada lado. A la derecha
habrá un pozo rodeado de yerbas, del que estará Cosme sacando un cubo de
agua, el que pondrá sobre el brocal, teniendo á su lado una regadera grande,
y entre las yerbas una brota. Cerca del pozo habrá una porcion de lechugas,
que se supone se acaban de arrancar. En este mismo lado se verá una puerta
abierta, que es por la que entran los de la poblacion á comprar legumbres.*

*A la izquierda y cerca de los bastidores, se verá la fachada interior de la
casa de Cosme, con puerta tambien abierta, y una reja pequeña, cubriendo
por encima á una, y á otra una parra frondosa. Rufino cabará con un hazadon
en lo último del foro, mirando alguna vez la puerta y reja de la casa con extremos de alegría. Por medio del foro se descubrirá el Sol que empieza á nacer,
el que irá subiendo é iluminando la escena por grados. Se oirá el agradable
cántico de las aves, y luego que Cosme á sacado y puesto el cubo sobre el
brocal, salen por la puerta de la huerta el Sargento y los tres soldados cantando
el quarto que sigue.*

The following is the set to act I of Zavala y Zamora's *El amor dichoso:*

*La Escena debe representar un monte con algunas quiebras y cabañas:
Amarili, y otras Pastoras y Pastores haciendo requeson, llenando algunos can-*

---

[15] See, for example, *El fabricante de paños, El trapero de Madrid, La Adelina,
El carbonero de Londres, El vinatero de Madrid, El amor perseguido, El naufragio
feliz* and *Eduardo y Federica* for other examples of elaborate *mise en scène.*

tarillos de leche, componiendo diversas flores en canastillos, ó adornando con cintas alguno que otro recental. Algunas ovejas paciendo sin órden por el monte. De su cinta baxará despeñado un riachuelo, habiendo en la parte más cómoda de él un puente rústico. A la izquierda de la Escena habrá una fuente con agua: junto á ella un álamo corpulento, y delante de él un poyo de piedra tosca. Toca la orqüestra una obertura estrepitosa, que calmará, con un solo agradable de flautas, y con él se abrirá la Escena. Descúbrese Dantéo sentado en un ribazo ó peña á orilla del rio, teniendo sobre sus rodillas un tierno recental, en cuya piel estará escribiendo con almagre los nombres de Dantéo y de Belisa.

El perfecto amigo is set in the outskirts of Munich:

> *El teatro debe representar una selva larga con un montecillo al frente: en su falda sobre los bastidores de la izquierda, un molino con puerta usual; y al pie del monte à la derecha, una encina corpulenta y poblada; y à la izquierda una choza rústica, tambien con puerta usual; de la cima del monte por la derecha baxa una cascada à comunicar sus aguas al molino. Al levantar el telon se descubren varios labradores apaleando castaña y bellota, y recogiéndola en sacos, que tendrán para este efecto; advirtiendo, que desde que se descubre la Escena, se dexarán ver algunos relámpagos à lo lexos, y de tarde en tarde, los quales serán mas continuados, y mas cerca. Algunos mozos del molino baxarán sucesivamente à la choza, y volverán à salir de ella con costales de trigo, que conducirán al molino.*

Even scenes of local color, future *cuadros de costumbres,* were evident in the comedia lacrimosa: see *La buena nuera, Las víctimas del amor, Ana y Sindhám, Cecilia viuda* and *La Cecilia,* the last with *canciones payas, bayletes con panderetas, seguidillas boleras* and *seguidillas a duo.* The vivid *tableaux* and detailed directions for pantomime also foreshadowed this trend in Romantic drama.

Martínez de la Rosa, a transitional playwright, spoke of the importance of visual effects to stimulate the sensibility of the audience.[16] External effects are extremely important in both *Aben Humeya* and *La conjuración de Venecia.*

Martínez de la Rosa, in an effort to evoke the time and place where *Aben Humeya* is set, gives detailed stage sets, impressive *tableaux* and scenes of local color complete with Moorish costumes, weapons, and instruments to accompany the songs and dances.

The same posturing and gesturing, typical of sentimental comedy, is found in *La conjuración de Venecia.* For example, in act III, scene i, *(Laura se dirige hacia la puerta por donde viene su padre, y al verle, faltanle las fuerzas y cae de rodillas.)* The *mise en scène* to act IV is spectacular:

> *El teatro representa la plaza de San Marcos, iluminada en el fondo el palacio ducal, en cuyos salones se ve circular la gente, resonando de tiempo en tiempo los ecos de la música; a la puerta una guardia.—En la plaza se descubren las*

---

[16] See his *Apuntes sobre el drama histórico* which were published with *La conjuración de Venecia* in 1834.

dos famosas columnas, y todo el ámbito aparece lleno de grupos de gente, paseándose y divirtiéndose, la mayor parte con máscaras y disfraces, así como los conjurados, y algunos soldados de la República.

Don Álvaro contains elaborately detailed stage-settings which show the appreciation of El duque de Rives, an artist, for the colorful, the realistic and the picturesque:

JORNADA PRIMERA

La escena es en Sevilla y sus alredededores

La escena representa la entrada del antiguo puente de barcas de Triana, el que estará practicable a la derecha. En primer término, al mismo lado, un aguaducho o barraca de tablas y lonas, con un letrero que diga: Agua de Tomares: dentro habrá un mostrador rústico con cuatro grandes cántaros, macetas de flores, vasos, un anafre con una cafetera de hoja de lata y una bandeja con azucarillos. Delante del aguaducho habrá bancos de pino. Al fondo se descubrirá de lejos parte del arrabal de Triana, la huerta de los Remedios con sus altos cipreses, el río y varios barcos en él, con flámulas y gallardetes. A la izquierda se verá en lontananza la Alameda. Varios habitantes de Sevilla cruzarán en todas direcciones durante la escena. El cielo demonstrará el ponerse el sol en una tarde de Julio, y al descorrerse el telón aparecerán: El Tío Paco detrás del mostrador en mangas de camisa; El Oficial, bebiendo un vaso de agua y de pie; Preciosilla, a su lado templando una guitarra; El Majo y los Dos Habitantes de Sevilla sentados en los bancos.

The *cuadros de costumbres* in this play not only serve a narrative purpose but also provide local color and comic relief from the intensity of the previous scenes. Several of these scenes sparkle with humor. The same can be said for the scenes of local color in *Don Juan Tenorio* and *El paje*.

Another example of a stage-set rich in detail can be found in the Romantic drama *Juan Lorenzo*.

ACTO PRIMERO

La accion pasa en Valencia en el año 1519

Sala baja en la casa de Juan Lorenzo. En el fondo, á la izquierda del actor, una pieza con grande entrada, y una cortina, que estará descorrida. Tambien en el fondo, y en el lado opuesto, una escalera, que comunica con las habitaciones del piso alto. Á la derecha, puerta y ventana, que dan á la calle, y á la izquierda la alcoba de Lorenzo. En el ángulo de la derecha, y pendientes de escarpias, algunos instrumentos del oficio de pelaire, y una espada. En la habitacion del fondo, un pequeño estante con libros, un retrato del cardenal Cisneros, una mesa y un sillon de baqueta; más hácia el proscenio, y cerca de la alcoba de Lorenzo, una mesa con algunos objetos de devocion, como cuadros con imágenes de santos, colocados contra la pared, y un crucifijo, alumbrado todo por una lámpara. Al levantarse el telon, estará Lorenzo en la habitacion del fondo, leyendo; otra lámpara arde sobre su mesa, aunque debe figurarse que es ya de dia.

133

IX. THE UNITIES: REINTERPRETATION OR VIOLATION?

Finally in its violation of the unities, Romantic drama found an important antecedent in the *comedia lacrimosa*. In its subordination of character to plot, sentimental comedy moves in the direction of Romantic drama. Sentimental comedy is fundamentally a drama of action. The pressure of time is constantly insisted upon.

Specific times are mentioned on eight different occasions in *El delincuente honrado* and underscore Torcuato's anguish as he awaits his execution. The rapidity with which *El precipitado* moves from scene to scene makes it a very fast moving drama. In *La Adelina* we also have the sensation of time passing quickly with constant mention of night and day, reminiscent of that famous line from *El Cid* «apriessa cantan los gallos e quieren crebar albores.» The constant and frequent changes of scene in *El amante honrado* suggest a rapid pace.

In general, the violations of the unities in sentimental comedy are slight. In his *Advertencia al lector* which accompanied the 1797 edition of *Las víctimas del amor, Ana y Sindhám,* Zavala y Zamora justified his loose interpretation of the unities: «la accion es una sola, aunque acompañada de varios accidentes. El lugar de la Escena se extiende á Londres y sus cercanias, ensanche que dió, y aun ha seguido en muchas composiciones la religiosidad de nuestros preceptistas Franceses. Solo la unidad del tiempo padece alguna violencia por la precipitacion de la catastrofe; pero el que conozca nuestros teatros, y sepa que mas se escrivió este drama para un público espectador que, para un sabio escrupuloso, disculpará esta y otras faltas en que haya incurrido.»

The unity of action is practically always observed. When subplots or scenes of local color are introduced, they relate to the main plot in a fundamental way. If the play does not occur within a period of twenty-four hours, it rarely goes beyond the following day. Such is the case in *El delincuente honrado:* the play begins at 7:40 A.M. one day and ends at 11:00 A.M. the following one. The unity of place is always liberally interpreted. Often there are many changes of place, but usually within the same city or general locale.

Martínez de la Rosa also wrote a defense of his use of the unities in *La conjuración de Venecia,* in his *Apuntes sobre el drama histórico.* His goal was to obtain «un justo medio»: «...poco reparo debe haber en mudar el lugar de la escena, antes que incurrir en tales faltas de verosimilitud que perjudiquen a la ilusión dramática mucho más que una o dos mudanzas de decoración ... creo que sobre este punto, así como sobre otros muchos, la verdad está en un justo medio ... Cada acto, como parte distinta y separada, puede muy bien suponerse acaecido en diverso lugar, sobre todo si no están entre sí muy distantes; ... Tampoco se debe regatear sobre el tiempo que se supone dura la acción: basta que lo que pasa a la vista de los espectadores pueda haber sucedido realmente en el mismo espacio, poco más o menos, y que lo restante del tiempo que ha tomado el poeta lo haya distribuído con tal sagacidad, especialmente entre los actos, que el espectador no se aperciba de ello o lo tolere de buen grado.»

Like all Romantic dramas, the play is very fast moving. The unity of action is observed, but the unities of time (five or more days) and place (five different sets but all in the same city) are interpreted very liberally, or perhaps one should say violated.

Alfredo is a drama of action, the pace being frenetic. All the action occurs on the island of Sicily, but within this area in a castle, on a mountain, and on a pass of another. We know that several days have passed in the course of the play from a speech Roberto makes in act IV, scene i.

Don Álvaro is the most exaggerated of all Spanish Romantic plays in its violation of the unities. The action shifts from Sevilla to Hornachuelos to Italy and back to the Convento de los Ángeles in the outskirts of Hornachuelos. Five years transpire in the course of the play. More than a year has passed when act II begins. And from a speech that Padre Guardián makes in the beginning of act V, we know that four years have gone by since the end of act III. Don Álvaro also refers to the fact that no one has come to see him in the four years he has lived as Padre Rafael. Finally, Don Alfonso informs Álvaro that he has been trying to locate his whereabouts for five years.

Larra, in his review of *El trovador,* spoke of the two principal actions of the play, but defended this violation by stating that both themes are perfectly blended and form a single, coherent and integrated dramatic action: «... en *El trovador* constituyen verdaderamente dos acciones principales ... una enterándonos del lance concerniente a la Gitana ... y otra poniéndonos al corriente del amor de Manrique, contrarrestado por el del conde, que constituye otra ... Estas dos acciones dramáticas ... se hallan, a pesar de la duplicidad, tan perfectamente enclavijadas, tan dependientes entre sí, que fuera difícil separarlas sin recíproco perjuicio.» [17] All the action occurs in Zaragoza and surroundings, but in various places—also outside (a gypsy cave, an encampment), and inside (in various rooms in the palace of Aljafería, in a convent). We know from Nuño, in the beginning of act II, that a whole year has passed since the end of act I.

El paje occurs in two different cities (Sevilla and Córdoba), shifting from site to site in each one. The action occurs during one day and part of a second.

Los amantes de Teruel takes place in two cities: Valencia and Teruel. Seven days transpire in the course of the play. Once again the action moves swiftly due to the circumstances of the plot. Marsilla had been given a period of time (six years and one week) by Don Pedro de Segura to gain fame and fortune as a means to obtain the hand of Don Pedro's daughter. When Marsilla first arrives on the scene, he announces how much time remains: «los anos ya / se cumplen hoy; cumplirá / el primer día mañana» (act I, scene iv). During the play the time pressure builds up and keeps the

[17] MARIANO JOSÉ DE LARRA, «El trovador,» in his *Artículos de costumbres* (Madrid: Espasa-Calpe, 1958), p. 124.

audience in suspense as to whether or not Marsilla, who has succeeded in obtaining wealth and fame, through heroic deeds, will arrive in time due to a set of hindrances contrived by the Moorish Queen of Valencia. This type of anxiety, due to the pressure of time, recalls *El delincuente honrado,* where we await the fatal hour when Torcuato is scheduled to be executed.

After *Los amantes de Teruel,* there is a stricter interpretation of the unities once again.

Doña Mencía takes place in Madrid in two different spots: in the home of Doña Mencía and in a convent. A year has passed between act II and III.

The action of *Alfonso el Casto* occurs within a single year, 792, and in two different locales: a monastery in Galicia and a church and a palace in Oviedo.

All the action in *Simón Bocanegra* occurs in Genova. As in *La conjuración de Venecia,* each act corresponds to a set change within the same general locale. The Prologue takes place in the year 1338; act I, twenty-four years later; and the subsequent acts within a period of two days.

The first four acts of *Don Juan Tenorio* take place in a single night. The three acts of Part II occur five years later and in another night. All the action takes place in Sevilla, although we find different spots within the same city.

Finally, in *Juan Lorenzo,* two or three days transpire in the course of the play and all the action takes place in Valencia, in either the home of Juan Lorenzo or in the patio of la Audiencia de Valencia.

EPILOGUE

This study has not been kind to the *comedia lacrimosa*. But while the plays could not be commended as drama, the genre itself and its transitional place between the Neo-classic and Romantic contains much that is of interest to the student of Spanish literature or of European literature and culture in general. It was that arch-Romanticist Percy Bysshe Shelley who called poets «the unacknowledged legislators of mankind,» and the most important word in that statement is «unacknowledged.» The lachrymose comedies aspired to legislate on a more direct route; but the relationship between art and society, and in societies where institutions tend to be more open, the relationsip between art and politics, is one of the most challenging and provocative areas for thought.

It must be left to other studies, but an examination of the relationship in time between didactic art forms such as the *comedia lacrimosa* and actual changes in specific customs and laws at which given works were aimed could be useful and provocative. There is a critical bias in this work that should be made explicit: didacticism makes poor art. But it is outside my area of competence to judge or answer other questions about didactic art or the particular genre under study here, for example: What was the effect of these plays on their audience? How wide was their circulation? What, if any, societal impact did they have?

The very fact that they were written tells us some very important things about Spanish society at that time. Laws and customs in European society up to the Age of the Enlightenment were creatures of, rather than concerns of, the upper classes. The themes of the *comedia lacrimosa* were middle-class as were their intended audience. But obviously, because of their goals, the middle-class, for whom these plays were written, was perceived as having power to effect change. In other words, their sentiment counted for something. The midde-class, much less a middle-class with influence and power to shape society, was such a new and important aspect of European life that if original attempts to exploit it in art were rather crude, we, looking back at these attempts should not only be understanding, but respesctful.

Because, above all, the plays brought together and studied in this book give us a chance to understand the aspirations of both artist and audience; and once again we see how closely we are linked in bonds of empathy to another time. It is this continuing discovery that justifies the rigors of inquiry.

BIBLIOGRAPHY

I

Comedias lacrimosas

The information enclosed within brackets below was obtained from Ada M. COE'S: *Catálogo bibliográfico y crítico de las comedias anunciadas en los periódicos de Madrid desde 1661 hasta 1819*; Emilio COTARELO Y MORI'S: *Isidoro Máiquez y el teatro de su tiempo*; GAYANGOS Y ARCE'S: *Catalogue of the Manuscripts in the Spanish Language in the British Museum*; I. L. MCCLELLAND'S: Bibliography in *Spanish Drama of Pathos*, II, and *The Origins of the Romantic Movement in Spain*; PALAU Y DULCET'S: *Manual del bibliotecario hispanoamericano*; and PAZ Y MELIÁ'S: *Catálogo de las piezas de teatro que se conservan en el departamento de manuscritos de la Biblioteca Nacional*. Unless otherwise specified, the editions I used contained no reference to place, publisher, or date.

Editions:	*Symbols and Abbreviations used in Quoting the Texts*
MS. *Cens.*	= Censors *(Censura)* manuscript copy.
Bar.	= Barcelona.
M.	= Madrid.
n.p.	= Place not known.
n.d.	= Date not known.
C.M.C.	= *Colección de las mejores comedias que van representando en esta corte*. Madrid, 1789.

Libraries:

B.M.	= British Museum, London.
B.M.P.	= Biblioteca Menéndez y Pelayo, Santander.
B. Mun.	= Biblioteca Municipal, Madrid.
B. Nac.	= Biblioteca Nacional, Madrid.

COMELLA Y VILLAMITJANA, Luciano Francisco: *Abuelo y la nieta, El*. [Bar., 1778 MS. *Cens.* 1792. B. Mun.]
— *Buena nuera, La*. [MS. *Cens.* 1794. B. Mun.], Barcelona: Juan Francisco Piferrer, n.d.
— *Cecilia, La*. Part I. [MS. *Cens.* 1786. B. Mun.]
— *Cecilia viuda, La*. Part II. [C.M.C. i (1789).]
— *Dos amigos, Los* [M.S. *Cens.* 1790. B. Mun.]
— *Hijo reconocido, El*. [M., n.d. (Pl. 1799) B. Mun.], Barcelona: Juan Francisco Piferrer, n.d.
— *Natalia y Carolina*. [MS. *Cens.* 1789. B. Mun.]
GIL Y ZÁRATE, Antonio: *Cecilia la cieguecita*. Madrid: Imprenta de Repullés, 1843.

139

JOVELLANOS, Gaspar Melchor de: *El delincuente honrado.* [Barcelona: Gilbert y Tutó ca. 1782; M., 1787; M., 1793], in *Obras de D. Gaspar Melchor de Jovellanos* B.A.E., XLVI, Madrid, 1951, pp. 82-100.

TRIGUEROS, Cándido María: *El precipitado.* [Entitled *Cándida o la hija sobrina* in the 1774 manuscript. B. Nac.], Sevilla: D. Manuel Nicolás Vázquez, D. Antonio Hidalgo y Compañía, 1785.

VALLADARES DE SOTOMAYOR, Antonio: *La Adelina.* [MS. *Cens.* 1781, B. Mun.], n.p., 1801.
— *Carbonero de Londres, El.* [?M. 1784; MS. B. Mun.], Barcelona, 1790.
— *Fabricante de paños, El.* [MS. Cens. 1783. B. Mun.]
— *Rufino y Aniceta.* [Author listed as D. Anastasio Valderosal y Montedoro—pseudonym—anagram of Valladares. B.M.P.], n.p., n.d.
— *Trapero de Madrid, El.* [MS. B. Mun.]
— *Vinatero de Madrid, El.* [M., 1784; M., 1787.]
— *Vivanderas ilustres, Las.* [M., 1792. B.M.], Barcelona: Juan Francisco Piferrer, n.d.

ZAVALA Y ZAMORA, Gaspar: *El amante generoso.* [?M., ?1790; MS. *Cens.* 1794. B. Mun.]
— *Amante honrado, El.* [n.p., ?1775; MS. *Cens.* 1793. B. Mun.]
— *Amor dichoso, El.* [?M., ?1790; n.p., n.d., B.M.]
— *Amor perseguido (El) y la virtud triunfante.* Cotarelo lists a perfomance on July 9, 1793 [MS. B. Mun.; M., 1792. B.M.]
— *Bueno y el mal amigo, El.* [Bar., n.d., n.p., ?1790; C.M.C. viii (1793).]
— *Eduardo y Federica.* [M.S. Cens. 1811. B. Mun.], Valencia: José Ferrer de Orga, 1817.
— *Naufragio feliz, El.* [?M., ?1790; Bar., n.d.; MS. *Cens.* 1782. B. Mun.]
— *Perfecto amigo, El.* [M.S. B. Mun.: M., 1790. B.M.], Barcelona: Pablo Nadal, 1798.
— *Triunfo del amor (El) y la amistad, Jenwal y Faustina.* [M., 1793; MS. 1804. B. Nac.], Valencia: Ildefonso Mompié, 1816.
— *Víctimas del amor (Las), Ana y Sindhám.* [MS. *Cens.* 1788. B. Mun.], Madrid: Don Antonio Cruzado, 1797. Coe says it was written as early as 1778.

II

Spanish Romantic Dramas

GARCÍA GUTIÉRREZ, Antonio. *Obras escogidas de*: Madrid: Imprenta y Estereotipia de M. Rivadeneyra, 1866.

    Juan Lorenzo, pp. 573-627.
    (El) Paje, pp. 31-58.
    Simón Bocanegra, pp. 191-241.
    (El) Trovador, pp. 1-30.

HARTZENBUSCH, Juan Eugenio: *Alfonso el Casto.* Madrid: Imprenta de Yenes, 1841.
— *(Los) Amantes de Teruel.* Madrid: Imprenta de Repullés, 1836.
— *Doña Mencía.* Madrid: Imprenta de Repullés, 1848.

LARRA, Mariano José de: *Macías,* in *La flor del teatro romántico.* Madrid: Ediciones Ibéricas, n.d., pp. 87-157.

MARTÍNEZ DE LA ROSA, Francisco: *Obras dramáticas.* Ed. Jean Sarrailh. *Clásicos Castellanos.* Madrid: Espasa-Calpe, 1964.

    Aben Humeya, pp. 119-230.
    (La) Conjuración de Venecia, pp. 233-336.

PACHECO, Joaquín Francisco: *Alfredo.* [Madrid: Tomás Jordan, 1835.]

RIVAS, Duque de: *Don Álvaro o la fuerza del sino,* in *La flor del teatro romántico.* Madrid: Ediciones Ibéricas, n.d., pp. 159-261.

ZORRILLA, José: *Don Juan Tenorio.* Colección Austral. Madrid: Espasa-Calpe, 1970, pp. 9-147.

III

English and French Sentimental Comedies

CIBBER, Colley: *Love's Last Shift;* or *The Fool in Fashion.* London: H. Rhodes, 1696.
DESTOUCHES, Philippe Néricault: *Les oeuvres de théâtre de Mr. Néricault Destouches.* 2 vols. Paris: François le Breton, 1716.
  (Le) Glorieux, II, pp. 1-118.
  (Le) Philosophe marié, II, pp. 1-110.
  [Although both plays are bound in the same volume II, they have separate pagination.]
DIDEROT, Denise: Oeuvres complètes. Ed. J. Assézat. Paris: Garnier Frères, 1875.
  (Le) Fils naturel, VII, 22-84.
  (Le) Père de famille, VII, 187-298.
LA CHAUSSÉE, Nivelle de: *Oeuvres.* 2nd ed., 1777; rpt. Geneva: Slatkine Reprints, 1970.
  (La) Fausse antipathie, pp. 15-36.
  Mélanide, pp. 114-151.
  (Le) Préjugé à la mode, pp. 42-68.
LILLO, George: *George Barnwell,* in *Modern British Drama.* 7 vols. London: William Miller, 1811. II, 71-91.
MOORE, Edward: *The Gamester,* in *Modern British Drama.* 7 vols. London: William Miller, 1811. II, 307-330.
SEDAINE, Michel-Jean: *Le Philosophe sans le savoir.* Paris: A. Hatier, 1929.
STEELE, Richard: *The Conscious Lovers.* London: J. Tonson, 1735.

IV

Scholarly and Critical Works Consulted

AGUILAR PIÑAL, Francisco: «La obra 'ilustrada' de don Cándido María Trigueros.» *Revista de Literatura,* 34, Nos. 67-68 (July-December, 1968), 31-56.
— *La Sevilla de Olavide 1767-1778.* Sevilla, 1966.
AIKEN, George A., ed.: *The Tatler.* 3 vols. New York: Hadley and Mathews, 1899.
BARBIER, J.-C.: *Les deux arts poétiques d'Horace et de Boileau.* Ed. Ernest Thorin. Paris: Librairie du Collège de France et de l'École Normale Supérieure, 1874.
BECCARIA, Cesare: *Dei delitti e delle pene.* Torino: Unione Tipografico-Editrice Torinese, 1911.
BENÍTEZ CLAROS, Rafael: «Variaciones sobre el sentimentalismo neoclásico.» *Visión de la literatura española.* Madrid: Ediciones Rialp, 1963, pp. 199-208.
BERNBAUM, Ernest: *The Drama of Sensibility: A Sketch of the History of English Sentimental Comedy and Domestic Tragedy 1696-1780.* Cambridge, Mass.: Harvard University Press, 1925.
— «The Romantic Movement.» *The English Romantic Poets: A Review of Research.* Ed. Thomas M. Raysor. New York: The Modern Language Association of America, 1950, pp. 1-37.
BOILEAU-DESPREAUX, Nicolas. *Épitres, Art poétique, Lutrin.* Paris; Sociéte les Belles Lettres, 1939.
BRUNETIÈRE, Ferdinand: «L'Évolution du drame bourgeois.» *Les époques du théâtre français (1636-1850)* 7th ed. Paris: Librairie Hachette, n.d., pp. 283-314.
BUTCHER, S. H., ed. and trans.: *Aristotle's Theory of Poetry and Fine Art.* New York: Dover Publications, 1951.
CAMPOS, Jorge: *Teatro y sociedad en España (1780-1820.)* Madrid: Editorial Moneda y Crédito, 1969.
CASO GONZÁLEZ, José M.: «El delincuente honrado, drama sentimental.» *La poética de Jovellanos.* Madrid: Prensa Española, 1972, pp. 193-234.
CAVE, Michael Robert: *La obra dramática de Luciano Francisco Comella.* Diss. University of Connecticut, 1972.

CHIAPPE, Andrew, ed., Benjamin BICKLEY ROGERS, trans.: *Five Comedies of Aristophanes*. New York: Doubleday and Co., 1955.

COE, Ada M.: *Catálogo bibliográfico y crítico de las comedias anunciadas en los periódicos de Madrid desde 1661 hasta 1819*. The Johns Hopkins Studies in Romance Literatures and Languages, Extra Vol. IX. Baltimore: The Johns Hopkins Press, 1935.

COLLIER, Jeremy: *A Short View of the Immorality and Profaneness of the English Stage*. 2nd ed., 1698; rpt. New York: Ams Press, 1974.

COOK, John A.: *Neo-classic Drama in Spain: Theory and Practice*. Dallas: Southern Methodist University Press, 1959.

COTARELO Y MORI, Emilio: *Isidoro Máiquez y el teatro de su tiempo*. Madrid: Imprenta de José Perales y Martínez, 1902.

DÉDÉYAN, Charles: *Rousseau et la sensibilité littéraire à la fin du XVIIIᵉ siècle*. Paris: Centre de Documentation Universitaire, 1966.

DESNOIRESTERRES, Gustave: *La comédie satirique au XVIIIᵉ siècle*. Paris: Librairie Académique Didier, 1885.

DIDEROT, Denise: *Oeuvres complètes*. Ed J. Assézat. Paris: Garnier Frères, 1875. VII.

— *Oeuvres esthétiques*. Paris: Éditions Garnier Frères, 1960.

ELOESSER, Arthur: *Das bürgerliche Drama: Seine Geschichte im 18. und 19. Jahrhundert*. 2nd ed.,, 1898; rpt. Geneva: Slatkine Reprints, 1970.

FEIJOO Y MONTENEGRO, Don Fr. Benito Gerónimo: *Cartas eruditas y curiosas*. 4 vols. Madrid: Real Academia de Derecho Español y Público, 1781, IV.

FERNÁNDEZ DE MORATÍN, Leandro: *Obras de Don Nicolás y de Don Leandro Fernández de Moratín*. B.A.E. II. Madrid, 1944.

— *Obras póstumas*. Madrid: Imprenta y Estereotipia de M. Rivadeneyra, 1868. III.

GAIFFE, Félix Alexandre: *Le Drame en France au XVIIIᵉ siècle*. 2nd ed., 1910; rpt. Paris: A. Colin, 1971.

GAYANGOS Y ARCE, Pascual de: *Catalogue of the Manuscripts in the Spanish Language in the British Museum*. 4 vols. London: William Clowes and Sons. 1875-93.

GOLDSMITH, Oliver: «An Essay on the Theatre; or, A Comparison between Laughing and Sentimental Comedy.» *Collected Works of Oliver Goldsmith*. Ed. Arthur Friedman. Oxford: Oxford University Press, 1966, III, 209-213.

HADAS, Moses: *A History of Greek Literature*. New York: Columbia University Press, 1950.

— *A History of Latin Literature*. New York: Columbia University Press, 1952.

HARRISON, G. B., ed.: *Major British Writers*. New York: Harcourt, Brace and Company, 1954.

HAZARD, Paul: *La Crise de la conscience européenne*. Paris: Boivin, 1935.

— *La Pensée européenne au XVIIIème siècle: De Montesquieu à Lessing*. Paris: Boivin, 1946.

JOVELLANOS, D. Gaspar Melchor de: *Obras*, B.A.E. XLVI. Madrid, 1951.

LANSON, Gustave: *Nivelle de la Chaussée et la comédie larmoyante*. 2nd ed., 1903; rpt. Geneva: Slatkine Reprints, 1970.

LARRA, Mariano José de: «El trovador.» *Artículos de costumbres*. Colección Austral. Madrid: Espasa-Calpe, 1958, pp. 123-127.

LENIENT, C.: *La Comédie en France au XVIIIᵉ siècle*. 2 vols. Paris: Librairie Hachette, 1888.

LUZÁN, Ignacio de: *La poética o reglas de la poesía en general y de sus principales especies*. Ed. Luigi de Filippo. Barcelona: Selecciones Bibliófilas, 1956. II.

— *Memorias literarias de París*. Madrid, 1751.

MARTIN, Frederick Carlyle: *The Dramatic works of Gaspar de Zavala y Zamora*. Diss. University of North Carolina, 1958.

MCCLELLAND, I. L.: *The Origins of the Romantic Movement in Spain: A Survey of Aesthetic Uncertainties in the Age of Reason*. 2nd ed., 1937; rpt. New York: Barnes and Noble Books, 1975.

— *Spanish Drama of Pathos (1750-1808)*. Toronto: University of Toronto Press, 1970. II.

NAVAS-RUIZ, Ricardo: *El romanticismo español: Documentos*. Madrid: Ediciones Anaya, 1971.

PALAU Y DULCET, Antonio: *Manual del bibliotecario hispanoamericano.* 26 vols. 2nd ed., 1923-1927; rpt. Barcelona: A. Palau, 1948-1972.

PAZ Y MELIÁ, Antonio: *Catálogo de las piezas de teatro que se conservan en el departamento de manuscritos de la Biblioteca Nacional.* 2nd ed., 1899; rpt. Madrid: Colegio Nacional de Sordomudos y de Ciegos, 1934. I.

PEAK, J. Hunter: *Social Drama in Nineteenth-Century Spain.* Chapel Hill: University of North Carolina Press, 1964.

POLT, John H. R.: *Gaspar Melchor de Jovellanos.* New York: Twayne Publishers, 1971.

— «Jovellanos' *El delincuente honrado.»* *Rom. Rev.,* L (1959), 170-190.

PRAZ, Mario: *The Romantic Agony.* New York: Meridian Books, 1956.

PREMINGER, Alexander, ed.: *Encyclopedia of Poetry and Poetics.* Princeton: Princeton University Press, 1965.

REYNAUD, Louis: *Le Romantisme: Les origines anglo-germaniques.* Paris: Librairie Armand Colin, 1926.

RICHARDSON, Samuel: *Clarissa Harlowe.* 4 vols. New York: E. P. Dutton and Co., 1932.

— *The History of Sir Charles Grandison.* 4 vols. Oxford: B. Blackwell, 1931.

— *Pamela,* or *Virtue Rewarded.* 4 vols. Oxford: B. Blackwell, 1929.

ROBERTSON, J. Logie, ed.: *The Complete Poetical Works of James Thomson.* London: Oxford University Press, 1908.

ROUSSEAU, Jean-Jacques: *Discours sur les sciences et les arts.* Ed. George R. Havens. New York: Modern Language Asso. of America, 1946.

— *Discours sur l'origine de l'inegalité.* Paris: Garnier-Flammarion, 1971.

— *Julie ou La Nouvelle Héloïse.* Paris: Éditions, Garnier Frères, 1960.

— *Lettre à d'Alembert sur les spectacles.* Ed. L. Brunel. Paris: Librairie Hachette, 1910.

— *Les Rêveries du promeneur solitaire.* Paris: Éditions Garnier Frères, 1960.

SARRAILH, Jean: «À Propos du *Delincuente honrado* de Jovellanos.» *Mélanges d'Études Portugaises Offerts à M. Georges Le Gentil.* Lisbon: Instituto Para a Alta Cultura, 1949, pp. 337-351.

SEBOLD, Russell P.: *Colonel Don José Cadalso.* New York: Twayne Publishers, 1971.

— «Enlightenment Philosophy and the Emergence of Spanish Romanticism.» *The Ibero-American Enlightenment.* Urbana: University of Illinois Press, 1971, pp. 111-140.

— «El incesto, el suicidio y el primer romanticismo español.» *Hispanic Review,* 41, No. 4 (Autumn, 1973), 669-692.

— *El rapto de la mente: Poética y poesía dieciochescas.* Madrid: Editorial Prensa Española, 1970.

— «Sobre el nombre español del dolor romántico.» *Insula,* No. 264. (November, 1968), 1, 4-5.

SHAFTESBURY, Earl of: *Characteristics of Men, Manners, Opinions and Times.* n.p., 1732.

   «An Inquiry Concerning Virtue, or Merit,» II, 5-176.
   «The Moralists, a Philosophic Rhapsody,» II, 181-443.

SILVA Y GÓNGORA, Pedro Francisco de: *Década epistolar sobre el estado de las letras en Francia.* 2nd ed., 1781; rpt. Madrid, 1792.

SMITH, Gregory, ed.: *The Spectator.* London: J. M. Dent and Sons, 1963. III.

SPELL, Jefferson Rea: *Rousseau in the Spanish World Before 1833: A Study in Franco-Spanish Literary Relations.* Austin: The University of Texas Press, 1938.

TOMPKINS, J. M. S.: *The Popular Novel in England, 1770-1800.* London, 1932.

VAN TIEGHEM, Paul: *Le Romantisme dans la littérature européenne.* Paris: Éditions Albin Michel, 1948.

VAN TIEGHEM, Philippe: *La Nouvelle Héloïse de Jean-Jacques Rousseau.* Paris: Société Française d'Éditions Littéraires et Techniques, 1929.

WILLEY, Basil: *The Eighteenth Century Background: Studies on the Idea of Nature in the Thought of the Period.* New York: Columbia University Press, 1950.

INDEX

145

146